T0167645

HOW TO TRACE YOUR
FAMILY TREE

Discover your personal roots and British heritage: everything from
accessing archives and public record offices to using the internet

KATHY CHATER

LORENZ BOOKS

This edition is published by Lorenz Books,
an imprint of Anness Publishing Ltd,
Blaby Road, Wigston,
Leicestershire LE18 4SE;

info@anness.com

www.lorenzbooks.com; www.annesspublishing.com

Anness Publishing has a new picture agency outlet for images for publishing,
promotions or advertising. Please visit our website www.practicalpictures.com
for more information.

Publisher: Joanna Lorenz
Editors: Joanne Rippin and Elizabeth Woodland
Cover Design: Nigel Partridge
Book design: Michael Morey

© Anness Publishing Ltd 2013

All rights reserved. No part of this publication may be reproduced, stored in a retrieval
system, or transmitted in any way or by any means, electronic, mechanical, photocopying,
recording or otherwise, without the prior written permission of the copyright holder.

A CIP catalogue record for this book is available from the British Library.

Previously published as part of a larger volume, *Family History Made Easy*

PUBLISHER'S NOTE
Although the advice and information in this book are believed to be accurate and true at
the time of going to press, neither the authors nor the publisher can accept any legal
responsibility or liability for any errors or omissions that may have been made nor for any
inaccuracies nor for any loss, harm or injury that comes about from following instructions
or advice in this book.

ACKNOWLEDGEMENTS
Reproduced by kind permission of: (l = left, r = right, m = middle, t = top, b = bottom)
Hugh Alexander: p24; p28 t; p36 t; p44; p46 t. Paul Anness: front cover tmr; p2 bl.
The Bridgeman Art Library: p17 br/Mallett & Son Antiques, UK; p21/Bristol City
Museum and Art Gallery, UK; p39/Private Collection; p53 b/Victoria & Albert Museum,
UK; p58/British Library; p62/Private Collection; p63 tr/Royal Geographical Society,
London; p66 b/John Bethell; p82/Guildhall Library; p82/Private Collection;
p88/Birmingham Museums and Art Gallery. The British Library: p46 b. The Church
of Jesus Christ of Latter-day Saints: p29 t; p30 t, bl, br; p33 ©2013 by Intellectual
Reserve, Inc. Used by permission. Barbara Clements: p2mt; p3 br. Corbis: p59 © Hulton-
Deutsch Collection; p66 t; p67; p72; p75; p76 t. Findmypast p35 r; Genuki p35 l; Guild of
One Name Studies p31 b; Mary Evans Picture Library: p7 tr; p42; p49 t; p50 tr, tl; p59 t;
p76 b; p77. Getty Images: p89. Sandra Hands: back cover bl, bmr; front cover main image,
bml; p1; p4 mb; p5 mt; p96 bl. Roots p34 l; Origins p34 r; Man Yee Woodland: back
cover tl, tml, bml, br; front cover bmr, br; p2 t, b; p3 t, mb; p96 tr.

Contents

Introduction

In today's increasingly globalized world, there is a desire to know more about ourselves as individuals and where we came from. As a result of this, family history is one of the fastest-growing hobbies.

This book is aimed at those who have British ancestry. There may be many other nations from which our forebears sprang, but, because British people (the English, the Welsh, the Scots, the Irish and the inhabitants of the many offshore islands that make up the United Kingdom) went to all the countries of the world, many of the world's billions of inhabitants have at least a drop of British blood in their veins.

Forty years of tracing my own family history and working professionally as a television researcher have taught me a great deal about how to find and use information. One of the most important things I have learned is that you don't have to be an expert at everything; instead, you need to be able to find an expert in the relevant field and then tap into his or her expertise. Luckily, the world of genealogy is full of knowledgeable and enthusiastic people who are generous with their help and experience. The current enthusiasm for the subject has also led to the appearance of a large number of magazines and publications, which provide further help for everyone from the total beginner to the highly experienced.

No single publication can hope to cover everything a family historian might need to

British people have always been great travellers for work, exploration or to settle.

Before the 20th century, this girl would have been lucky to see her second birthday.

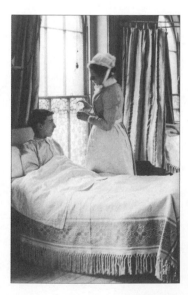

Nursing is a well regulated profession, with excellent records that make it easy to research.

The children around this table in the early 1950s may have grown up to live and work all over the world.

Members of the armed forces may have brought brides from overseas back home to Britain.

know. The researcher needs to be aware of what the law was at a particular time and how legal changes would be reflected in records produced by the government and private organizations, which is what I have concentrated on here. This will help genealogists find out in the most interesting way how their ancestors contributed to their community and the wider world.

Abbreviations

Genealogy has a host of abbreviations and acronyms. The main ones used in the text are:

BMD = births, marriages and deaths

CMB = christenings, marriages and burials

CRO = County Record Office

DRO = Diocesan Record Office

FFHS = Federation of Family History Societies

FHP = Family History Partnership

GRO = General Register Office

IGI = International Genealogical Index

IHGS = Institute of Heraldic and

Genealogical Studies

LDS = Church of Jesus Christ of Latter-day Saints (Mormons)

LMA = London Metropolitan Archives

PCC = Prerogative Court of Canterbury

PCY = Prerogative Court of York

PRO = Public Record Office, now known as TNA, see below

PRONI = Public Record Office of Northern Ireland

SRO = Scottish Record Office

SoG = Society of Genealogists

TNA = The National Archives, previously known as the PRO

Many people, like this Italian ice-cream seller, settled in Britain because of political or economic factors.

First Steps

We all wonder sometimes about the chain of events that led to us being alive here and now, and which characters and actions made us the people we are. Let us now take the first steps to finding out who we are and where we came from.

How to begin

There are several things that can spark off an interest in tracing a family's history. Sorting out possessions after a death, or when selling a family home usually reveals certificates, photographs and other mementos that give tantalizing clues to past joys and sorrows. Often these will be the starting point for a journey back in time.

A great deal of information can be gained from these items, and this, in turn, will give clues to further avenues of research. The first thing to do, therefore, is to sift through what you have found, concentrate on one particular individual, and use this information to create an outline of his or her life. Study these possessions to see if you can glean when and where the person was born, went to school, worked, married, etc. Dates and other information may come from what was written or inscribed on the items, but sometimes, especially with pictures (either photographs or movies), this can only be inferred from the content.

Interpreting the evidence

Among the treasured possessions found in an ancestor's home, you might find some of the following items:

- certificates (birth, marriage, death, adoption, baptism, confirmation)
- photographs and drawings
- home movies
- correspondence (letters and postcards)
- scrapbooks
- diaries
- household and/or business accounts books
- insurance policies
- newspaper cuttings
- family bibles and prayer books
- apprenticeship indentures
- books presented as prizes or inscribed to commemorate a special event
- examination or school-leaving certificates
- identity cards
- ration books (rationing in Britain started in World War II and continued until 1955)
- medals, badges and other objects connected with service in the armed forces
- membership of clubs or organizations such as friendly societies or the Freemasons
- passports
- holiday or travel souvenirs
- retirement presents
- memorial cards
- wills and other legal documents

D

F. No. 4058

THESE are to certify, That Florence Daughter of William Edward Nightingale and Frances his Wife, who was Daughter of Wm. Smith Esq. M.P was Born in in the Parish of in the City of Florence the twelfth of Day of May in the Year eighteen hundred and twenty at whose Birth we were present.

Frances Gale

[illegible]

57

Registered at Dr. Williams's Library, Redcross Street, near Cripplegate, London.

July 12th 1820 Thos. Morgan Registrar.

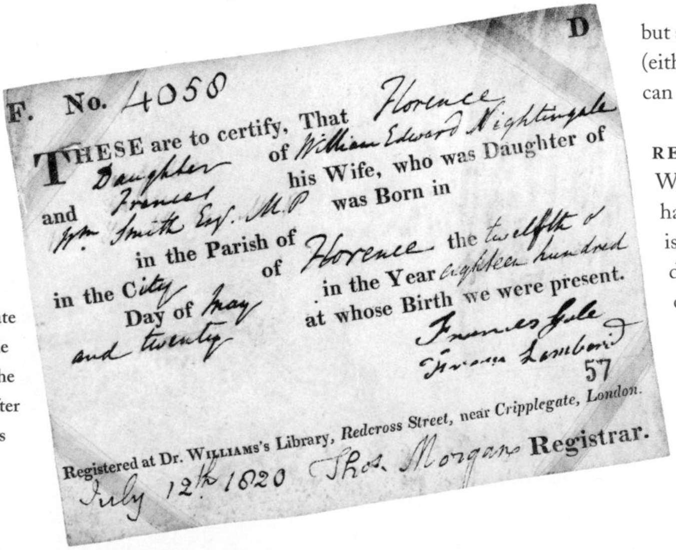

RIGHT Florence Nightingale's birth certificate shows that she was born in the Italian city after which she was named.

RECORDING YOUR FINDINGS

Write down all the information you have found in chronological order. It is a good idea to use a piece of paper divided into two columns. The first column, which should occupy about two-thirds of the page, is where you write the information gained; the other is for a note of its source. On another piece of paper, write down all the questions that are raised.

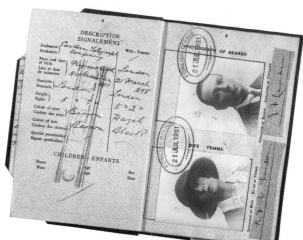

LEFT This early photo was taken c.1840. The dress and hairstyle give clues to the date.

RIGHT A passport issued in 1921. Were the couple going abroad for a holiday or to work?

BELOW A couple sign the wedding register in 1947.

ABOVE You may find you remember hearing stories relating a relative. Write these down too (but bear in mind that they may not be accurate).

INVESTIGATING FAMILY MYTHS

Many families have myths and legends about their origins. These usually contain a nugget of truth, but it has probably been distorted over the centuries.

"We came over with William the Conqueror" is a common family myth. Although you will probably find out that your ancestor did not arrive in England from France in 1066 with William the Conqueror, you may discover that you do indeed have French ancestry: perhaps a Huguenot fleeing religious persecution in the 16th or 17th century, or someone escaping from the Reign of Terror that followed the French Revolution in the 18th century. More prosaically, perhaps, your ancestor may prove to be a French sailor who deserted his ship, perhaps smitten by the charms of a British girl.

Other stories, on further research, may prove to be not quite so romantic. Those with Irish ancestry, for example, may be told that their ancestors were

heroes transported for political activity. Further research may indicate, however, that the Irish person was in fact transported for a squalid murder or theft, with no glamorous or political circumstances at all.

Another common family myth is illegitimate descent from a noble family. There are very few families who do not have an illegitimate child in their history, but often the story about aristocratic connections is just that – a tale concocted to make a child feel better about his or her fatherless state.

Family history is frequently full of surprises, some pleasant but others less agreeable. When doing research, you have to be prepared for both types.

BELOW This family shot was taken in 1947. Where are all the children now and do they have any useful documents or information?

CHOOSING A NAME TO RESEARCH

It is worth giving some thought to the branch of your family with which you decide to begin your research. Most people begin with their own family surname, but as your first steps into research should be regarded as practising, you should try to make your task as easy as possible. Therefore there are two major factors to consider before deciding which name and which family branch to research: the name and the location.

Name If you have a very common name, such as Smith, Jones or Brown,

you may be setting yourself too hard a task to begin with. An unusual name is far easier to extract from records.

Location London is the location of the major repositories, such as the The National Archives (TNA), the Society of Genealogists' (SoG) library, a number of County Record Offices (CROs) local studies libraries and other archives, so you might think that a London ancestor would be a good starting point. The problem with London, however, is that there are so many places where records relating to your ancestor might be located. Londoners were highly mobile, and a

BELOW If one of your grandmothers had a more unusual maiden name than the other, it will be easier to track their relatives.

ABOVE A professional portrait like this may have a studio address on the back that will give a clue to the sitter's location.

BELOW The exotic background of this picture is a photographer's set, not an indication that the girl was born abroad.

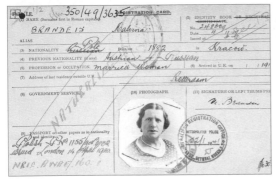

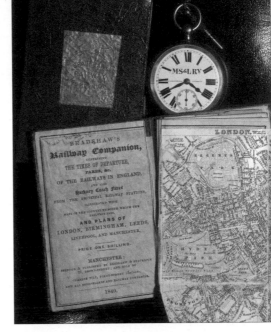

ABOVE Malvina Brandeis's unusual name will make finding references to her easy, but, as she was born abroad, tracing her ancestors is too hard at this stage.

ABOVE This guard's pocket watch and the railway guide will give clues to an ancestor's job.

house move of only a few hundred metres (yards) might mean that you have to shuttle between one record office and another. Moving from north to south of the river before 1888 also means changing the CROs and Diocesan Record Offices (DROs) that you will be using (there are at least seven covering different parts of the Greater London area).

If you do not live in London yourself, you will probably spend as much time travelling as you will researching. In addition, you will often find that records in London give much less detail than those elsewhere in Britain. Clerks in the capital were busy and did not know as much about the people who appeared before them as they did in a small neighbourhood.

Tracing ancestors in a smaller city, town or village can be easier. Each county usually has one main record office for all the places in it (although there may be small, local archives). This means that, even if your ancestor moved 32 km (20 miles), as long as he did not cross a county boundary, you will usually find the records in the same place. There are also less voluminous records to search in a small place. Going through the registers of some London parishes can occupy a whole wearisome day, while those in a rural town or village may take only a couple

BELOW Postcards sent home from the front will show where a fiancée was living before marriage.

of hours. Even names that would be common in a town or city, such as Wood or King, may be rare in a small place, which means that you can be fairly sure that all those of the same name are potentially related.

If you are not doing the research yourself and are planning to hire someone to do it for you, consider how much time all this record searching will take and whether you are prepared to pay for it.

FURTHER HELP

Foy, Karen *Ancestors in the Attic* (The History Press)

Family photographs

Photographs of family members not only allow us to debate just who has inherited Great-grandmother's eyes or Uncle Charlie's nose, they also allow us to put faces to the names on official and unofficial documents. There may also be clues in the photographs which will suggest further avenues of research.

COLLECTING PHOTOGRAPHS

Get copies of as many family photographs as you can. Needless to say, if any of them are borrowed, make sure that you return them in good condition. If you need to send them, package them safely and use a secure, insured form of delivery. Ideally, though, they should be returned in person. This has the additional benefit of giving time in which both you and

---

Interpreting photographs

It is, unfortunately, rare to find that your ancestors have written the date of the photograph, where it was taken and the names of all the people in it on the back. (Note that this is a lesson for you to learn about your own prints.) Even if you can identify the people, it may be difficult to estimate the date, though clues include:

- the clothes or uniforms the people were wearing

- the approximate ages of any children in the picture (children's ages are easier to guess than adults')
- cars or other methods of transport, such as bicycles or trains
- shops or other buildings
- the name of the photographer stamped on the back
- the type of photographic process used

BELOW This photograph was taken in Northamptonshire around 1900. The grandfather's jacket suggests a countryman.

the owner of the photograph may have thought of other things to discuss.

There are commercial companies that will copy photographs for you. They usually advertise in family history magazines, or you can look for them in local telephone directories. If a member of your family is a good photographer, you can get them photographed directly. They easiest way to do it today, however, is to scan them into your computer.

CLOTHES

People usually dressed up in their best to have their photograph taken. The clothes will therefore be their newest and most fashionable. A book on the history of costume should help you to identify roughly when the photograph was taken. Poor people, however, would not necessarily dress in the height of fashion. Employers often passed on their clothes to their servants, and many people could afford to dress only in second-hand garments. People dressed in the uniforms of the armed services were often either just joining up or about to go away to war, which might give a clue to the year. As well as estimating the date, you can get a lot of information from the uniform itself. From the style of the uniform, the cap, badges, medals and other insignia you get clues to identify which service they served in, their rank and their regiment, ship or squadron, if you don't already know this from other sources.

Other uniforms can help you to find out what members of your family did. Policemen, postmen, lifeboatmen, bus conductors, hospital nurses and a host of other people all had different uniforms depending on where they worked. Lawyers and judges still wear different styles of wig. You may also find an ancestor wearing the regalia of a Freemason.

Even if your ancestors did not wear the formal uniform of a particular organization, you may get clues about their job from what they wore. It was far easier in the past to tell occupations from clothes than it is today. Many people wore aprons: parlour maids

LEFT A group of nurses pictured where they worked. Unfortunately, the photo is too small to offer any clues about where this might be.

BELOW LEFT Three Air Force pilots in Canada in 1941. The shot's informality shows they were on leave rather than on duty.

usually wore decorative ones, while maids-of-all-work wore much rougher coveralls; butchers' aprons were striped; carpenters' aprons had pockets to hold tools, and woodworkers wore a special side apron with a breastpad to protect their chests. The smocks of farm workers had different motifs and styles depending on what kind of work they did and the area they came from. Fishermen's sweaters also had different motifs, often unique to them, so that bodies washed up after accidents at sea could be identified. All these can be researched through books.

BUILDINGS

If you have a photograph taken outside a shop and the name is visible, you can find out how long it was in business by using street directories. The same applies to pictures taken outside a nursing home, perhaps of a group of nurses that includes your ancestor. If you know in which town it would have been, a street directory will help you to identify the place, and by looking through different years you can find out how long it was in existence there, which will give you dates between which the photograph might have

been taken. Books on transport will also help you to date cars or other vehicles in the photograph.

PHOTOGRAPHERS AND THEIR PHOTOGRAPHS

Street directories will also enable you to locate the photographer who took the picture, if the name is stamped on it. By looking through a succession of years, you can narrow down how long the photographer was in business. The photographic method used can also give clues, but you will need to consult an expert about this.

FURTHER HELP

Pols, Robert *Family Photographs 1860-1945* (PRO)
Pols, Robert *Dating Old Army Photographs* (FHP)
Shrimpton, Jayne *Family Photographs and How to Date Them* (Countryside Books) *How to Get the Most from Family Pictures* (Society of Genealogists)
Storey, Neil *Military Photographs & How to Date Them* (Countryside Books)
Swinnerton, I. *Identifying Your World War I Soldier from Badges and Photographs* (FFHS)

A basic family tree

From the very earliest stages of your research, you should find information that, combined with your own family knowledge, can be used to draw up a basic family tree. There are a number of ways in which you can record what is called a pedigree, which is the technical term for an outline showing descent from an ancestor. Computer programmes and websites that help record family history have the facility to print out pedigrees, often in different formats. The various ways of doing this have advantages and disadvantages.

PREPARING A DROP-LINE CHART
The most common way of drawing up a basic family tree, and the method with which most people are familiar, is the drop-line chart.

Notes
- Group each of the generations on the same level.
- Put men/husbands on the left and women/wives on the right.

- Put children in the order of their birth, oldest on the left, not (as was sometimes done in the past) all the boys first and then all the girls.
- Show children descending from the marriage or relationship of two people, not from the father or mother. Legitimate children are

ABOVE A pedigree of King James I, prepared *c*.1605, shows his descent from various Scottish kings and also the god Wodan. Accuracy cannot be relied on.

BELOW A drop-line chart shows descent from a single couple and contains only one family line.

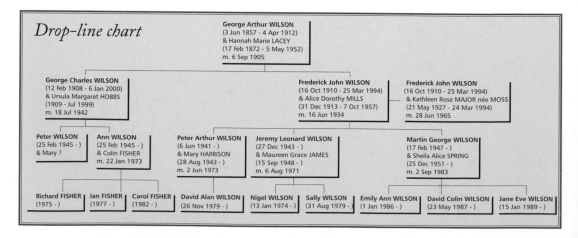

Drop-line chart

George Arthur WILSON
(3 Jun 1857 - 4 Apr 1912)
& Hannah Marie LACEY
(17 Feb 1872 - 5 May 1952)
m. 6 Sep 1905

George Charles WILSON
(12 Feb 1908 - 6 Jan 2000)
& Ursula Margaret HOBBS
(1909 - Jul 1999)
m. 18 Jul 1942

Frederick John WILSON
(16 Oct 1910 - 25 Mar 1994)
& Alice Dorothy MILLS
(31 Dec 1913 - 7 Oct 1957)
m. 16 Jun 1934

Frederick John WILSON
(16 Oct 1910 - 25 Mar 1994)
& Kathleen Rose MAJOR née MOSS
(21 May 1927 - 24 Mar 1994)
m. 28 Jun 1965

Peter WILSON
(25 Feb 1945 -)
& Mary ?

Ann WILSON
(25 Feb 1945 -)
& Colin FISHER
m. 22 Jan 1973

Peter Arthur WILSON
(6 Jun 1941 -)
& Mary HARRISON
(28 Aug 1943 -)
m. 2 Jun 1973

Jeremy Leonard WILSON
(27 Dec 1943 -)
& Maureen Grace JAMES
(15 Sep 1948 -)
m. 6 Aug 1971

Martin George WILSON
(17 Feb 1947 -)
& Sheila Alice SPRING
(25 Dec 1951 -)
m. 2 Sep 1983

Richard FISHER
(1975 -)

Ian FISHER
(1977 -)

Carol FISHER
(1982 -)

David Alan WILSON
(26 Nov 1979 -)

Nigel WILSON
(13 Jan 1974 -)

Sally WILSON
(31 Aug 1979 -)

Emily Ann WILSON
(1 Jan 1986 -)

David Colin WILSON
(23 May 1987 -)

Jane Eve WILSON
(15 Jan 1989 -)

shown by a solid line, illegitimate ones by a broken line.

- Put multiple marriages in order, left to right, and write the number against each one.
- Write the details of the marriage under the mother's name.
- Try not to cross lines of descent. This can be difficult if cousins marry and their descendants also marry, but with careful planning it should be possible.
- Do not include more than one branch of the family in the chart or it will soon become too big and unwieldy to use easily.
- Draw up a different chart for each branch, though this may be impossible where you find that different branches are descended from the same people through relatives marrying each other. When this happens, you may have to break some of these rules to fit it all in, especially if the people who marry are from different generations.

Uncles, aunts and cousins

The drop-line chart method is particularly useful for working out family relationships.

The types of relationship that sometimes give people trouble include great-aunts and great-uncles. In the diagram shown on the right:

- A and B are siblings.
- A is D's aunt/uncle; D is A's niece/nephew.
- A is F's great-aunt/uncle; F is A's great-niece/nephew.
- A is H's great-great-aunt/uncle; H is A's great-great-niece/nephew.

Cousinship is something else that gives people problems, especially when getting into the realm of second/third/fourth, etc., and trying to sort out who is a first/second cousin "removed". The rules, in fact, are very simple:

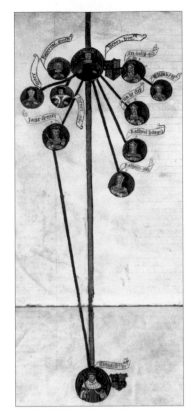

ABOVE A pedigree of Henry VIII, his six wives and their offspring. His son, the future Edward VI, is joined by a thick line.

BELOW Sorting out relationships can be complicated, but this chart should help.

- First cousins have the same set of grandparents.
- Second cousins have the same great-grandparents.
- Third cousins have the same great-great grandparents.

(The quick method is to count the number of "greats" and then add one to get the degree of cousinship.) Cousins are of the same generation, but not necessarily of similar age. When you want to work out the relationship between cousins who are "removed", i.e. who are not of the same generation, you need to go to the generation line on the family tree of the person from the younger generation, and then to move up to the generation of cousinship. In the diagram below, E is the first cousin once removed of D, because E's parent C is D's cousin. E's child G is the first cousin twice removed of D, because G is of the second generation below. G is the second cousin once removed of F, because E is F's second cousin and G is one generation below. Note that cousinship can be removed only upwards, i.e. F is not G's second cousin once removed.

This level of information can seem confusing, but in diagram form can become quite easily discernable.

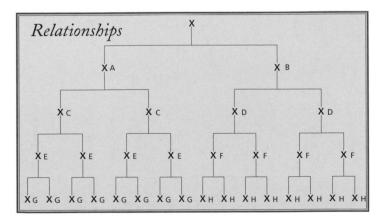

Relationships

CHOOSING ANOTHER METHOD

Alternative formats for beginning to build up a visual representation of your family tree to the drop-line chart include the birth brief, the narrative indented tree and the concentric tree.

Once you have gathered a substantial amount of information about your ancestors, you might want to construct a more elaborate chart for display; there are many decorative charts available, both as printed copy and on CD-rom. The computerized versions are obviously more flexible as you can add or change information as you go.

The birth brief

This is a simple chart that is useful when you are first starting out. The birth brief is a representation of only the direct ancestors of one individual and it usually includes only the last four generations. Brothers, sisters and any second or third marriages are omitted. The format of a birth brief is similar to a drop-line chart, it simply holds less information.

The narrative indented tree

This is the method used for publications such as *Burke's Peerage* or *Debrett's*. It does allow lots of children to be included, but it can be a bit confusing to find your way around. Each generation is assigned a number or letter, and the children of a couple are listed with details of their marriages and, indented, their children. It is

RIGHT When you see "of whom presently" (last line) this means that the descent of that person has been written out elsewhere and a new line of descent started for him/her.

BELOW The birth brief shows direct descent and does not include siblings.

important to make sure that every person has a unique number that applies only to him/her, so the tree requires very careful drafting. A lot of information can be packed into less space, so it is worth considering this style when you have done a great deal of research. You also need to be familiar with this type of tree in case the pedigree of any of your relations appears in such books.

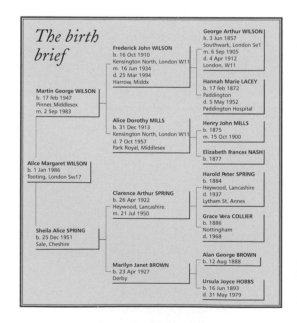

The birth brief

Martin George WILSON
b. 17 Feb 1947
Pinner, Middlesex
m. 2 Sep 1983

Frederick John WILSON
b. 16 Oct 1910
Kensington North, London W11
m. 16 Jun 1934
d. 25 Mar 1994
Harrow, Middx

George Arthur WILSON
b. 3 Jun 1857
Southwark, London Se1
m. 6 Sep 1905
d. 4 Apr 1912
London, W11

Hannah Marie LACEY
b. 17 Feb 1872
Paddington
d. 5 May 1952
Paddington Hospital

Alice Dorothy MILLS
b. 31 Dec 1913
Kensington North, London W11
d. 7 Oct 1957
Park Royal, Middlesex

Henry John MILLS
b. 1875
m. 15 Oct 1900

Elizabeth Frances NASH
b. 1877

Alice Margaret WILSON
b. 1 Jan 1986
Tooting, London Sw17

Clarence Arthur SPRING
b. 26 Apr 1922
Heywood, Lancashire.
m. 21 Jul 1950

Harold Peter SPRING
b. 1884
Heywood, Lancashire
d. 1937
Lytham St. Annes

Grace Vera COLLIER
b. 1886
Nottingham
d. 1968

Sheila Alice SPRING
b. 25 Dec 1951
Sale, Cheshire

Marilyn Janet BROWN
b. 23 Apr 1927
Derby

Alan George BROWN
b. 12 Aug 1888

Ursula Joyce HOBBS
b. 16 Jun 1893
d. 31 May 1979

The narrative indented tree

William Williamson b 1840, Rector of Chawleigh Regis, Somerset, m 1868 Harriet Peel (2nd dau of James and Elizabeth Peel of Edinburgh), d 1903 and had issue:

1   William b & d 1869
2   Harriet b 1870 d 1880
3   Thomas b 1871, took holy orders, m 1891 Sophia Ann Bristow, d 1950 and had issue
   a   Thomas William b 1891 Fellow of St Chad's College, Cambridge, m 1922 Olive Johnson, d 1949 and had issue
      i   Julia Mary b 1923
      ii   Ann Elizabeth b 1925 m 1950 Christopher St John Lucas, Esq.
      iii   Christine Ann b 1929 m 1949 Percy Arthur Black
   b   George Frederick b 1893 m 1918 Ivy Kavanagh and had issue
      i   Percival Thomas William b 1925 m 1952 Joyce Lewis
   c   Cyril Edward b 1895, sub-lieutenant on HMS Dragon, d 1916
4   George b & d 1872
5   Charles b & d 1872
6   James b 1875, headmaster of Bellingham School, Somerset m 1900 Mary Ann Weston (elder dau of the Hon. Roderick and Lavinia Gascoigne-Hunter), d 1962 and had issue
   a   Sarah Catherine b 1902
   b   John James b 1904 d 1915
   c   Leonard Thomas b 1906 m 1930 Elizabeth Mary James (only dau of Alexander and Aileen McKellan), d 1990 and had issue
      i   Marian Mary b 1931
      ii   Kenneth Thomas b 1935
   d   Ronald Albert b 1909, m 1928 Jessica McDonald and had issue
      i   Roderick James b 1928 m. 1955
   e   Ethel Rosamund b 1913 m 1933 Professor William Goldblatt
7   John b 1877 of whom presently

The concentric tree

This is useful to show, at a glance, your direct descent from all the different branches of your family. Your details (or those of your children) are placed in the centre. In the next circle appear the father and mother: father at the top and mother at the bottom. The one after is used for the central individual's grandparents, and so on.

The problem with this method is that, because the most distant ancestors appear in the outer sections, where there is more space, annoying gaps can soon open up. However, this kind of chart makes a decorative picture and a good instant reference that

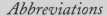

Abbreviations

Whatever form of chart you use, you will find the following abbreviations vital both to record your own information in a concise manner and to understand the information you find in existing charts.

b. born
bp. baptized
m. married individual
= shows a marriage. There are different ways to show illegitimacy: some people use ≠ to show that the couple were not married but either cohabited or had children.
mar. marriage
diss. dissolved (i.e. divorce)

▼ a downward arrow shows that the couple had a child or children but that they are not included
d. died
d.yng. died young
bur. buried
dsp. died without issue (from English/Latin died *sine prole*)
c. about (from Latin *circa*) in front of an approximate date
fl. flourishing (i.e. was alive) before a date
MI memorial inscription (used to show there is a gravestone or a memorial in a church/chapel/temple, etc.)
Will prov. A will has been proved

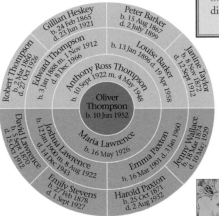

ABOVE The concentric tree puts the most recent generation at the centre. It does not include siblings.

you can hang in your home or give to relatives as a present, but it is best prepared when you have done a good deal of research.

Decorative charts

The other kinds of pictorial and decorative charts that are available to record your family tree are ideal for the culmination of your research, and make perfect special gifts for relatives.

BELOW Not everyone has quite so flourishing a family tree as Queen Victoria. This kind of chart is decorative but not much use in sorting out relationships.

FURTHER HELP

McLaughlin, Eve *Laying Out a Pedigree* (McLaughlin Guides)
Palgrave-Moore, Patrick *How to Record Your Family Tree* (Elvery Dowers Publications)

Names

Researching names can tell us a great deal about our families and their histories. Surnames may reveal where a family originated or what an ancestor did for a living, or it may be a patronymic or nickname. First names, too, can suggest regional links.

UNDERSTANDING NAMING PATTERNS

As you draw up your first family tree, you may notice naming patterns emerging. In the past it was common to call the first child after a parent or grandparent. Second or subsequent names might also be given in honour of a member of the family or to preserve the mother's maiden name. This is how many double-barrelled surnames originated.

Naming children after relatives means that a family might share a small pool of names. For men the most common names were John, William, Henry and Thomas, for women Elizabeth, Mary, Ann/e and Sarah. In the 17th century, biblical names were common, the 18th century brought a fashion for classical names, and in the 19th century Old English names were revived. The name of the current monarch was always a popular choice.

There were also names that had only local popularity. A daughter called Frideswide (sometimes Frideswith), for example, suggests that the family had connections with Oxford, since the cathedral there is built over the remains of an early English saint of that name who founded a convent. Used in the 19th or 20th century, it may suggest that the family were Catholics. Loveday, given originally to

ABOVE Until the 20th century, it was common to call subsequent children by the same name as a deceased child in order to make sure that the name continued in the family.

both boys and girls but later to girls only, suggests Cornish links, while Marmaduke, which was popular in the north, particularly Yorkshire, was rare in the rest of Britain.

THE HISTORY OF SURNAMES

Before the Middle Ages, people had only one name; it was only in the 13th century that surnames began to be used in England. These names seem to have been developed from four different sources: places, occupations, nicknames and patronymics.

Place names

These can be a large town such as Chester, or a village such as Oulton, which is the name given to four different places in Cumbria, Norfolk, Suffolk and Yorkshire. They may also come from a local landmark, such as Ditchfield, Atwell, or Wood. It is

worth looking up your surname in an atlas or dictionary of place names to see if it comes from a small village.

Occupations

Names such as Smith, Baker, Glover (glove maker) or Fletcher (arrow maker) show that your ancestor played an important part in the economy of his community. A skilled woman among your forebears will have left a surname ending in "-ster", such as Brewster (a female brewer) or Collister (a female collier – a charcoal burner or seller). We call unmarried women "spinsters" because they earned their living by spinning wool – a major source of England's wealth in the Middle Ages. Some of these surnames, such as Faber, meaning a smith, have French or Latin origins. When surnames were introduced, Norman French and Latin were both used by officials.

Nicknames

In these politically correct times it would be unthinkable to call someone Cruikshank (crooked legs), but our ancestors had a much rougher sense of humour. Other names record personal eccentricities, such as Pennyf(e)ather, meaning a miser.

Patronymics

This means a name derived from the name of the person's ancestor or father, such as the son of John being called Johnson, and that of William being called Williamson. Robinson and Wilson preserve pet names for men named Robert or William. Some women are also commemorated in names such as Allison (Alice's son) or Widowson, which may show that an ancestor was illegitimate or posthumous (born after the father died).

Celtic surnames

The Celtic countries (Wales, Scotland and Ireland) adopted surnames much later than England, and they generally

ABOVE Younger children often received more fashionable names than older siblings.

used patronymics. In Welsh, "ap" means "son of", but the first vowel disappeared, producing names such as Price (ap Rhys), Pritchard (ap Richard) or Prothero, a variant of Prydderch (ap Rydderch). Such names therefore indicate Welsh origins. A fixed surname here was not common until the 18th century. As an alternative to putting "ap" at the beginning or "son" at the end of the father's name, the Welsh often simply added "s", so names such as Edwards (son of Edward) and Jones (son of John) are common there.

Cornwall, another major Celtic area in England, also tended to use the father's name, though with no prefixes or suffixes. The Cornish also started using a fixed surname much later than the rest of the country. George, for example, did not become a common name until the Hanoverian kings, who started in 1714, long after the majority of surnames in England were formed, so someone with the surname George or John or Thomas should suspect Cornish or Welsh origins.

"Mac" or "Mc" means "son of", so the Macdonalds, the McCraes and the Macmillans have Scottish ancestry, but some of the Mcs, such as McNulty or McMullan, are of Irish origin. (Both the Scots and Irish spoke Gaelic.)

The purely Irish equivalent of the patronymic is "O", as in O'Casey and O'Neill. Sometimes the "O" was dropped, giving just "Casey" or "Neill".

Although patronymics were the most common method of surname formation in the Celtic countries, place names and nicknames were also used.

Uncommon surnames

Although the majority of surnames were, in England at least, fixed by the mid-13th century, and so preserve what was normal in the medieval

FURTHER HELP

Hanks, Patrick and Hodges, Flavia *A Dictionary of First Names* (OUP) (An earlier version of this book, *The Oxford Dictionary of English Christian Names* by E.G.W. Withycombe, is in some ways more useful to the family historian because it includes historical information about the use of names in documents and other sources.)
Mills, A.D. *A Dictionary of English Place Names* (OUP)
Reaney, P.H. and Wilson, R.M. *Dictionary of English Surnames* (OUP)
Titford, John *Penguin Dictionary of Surnames* (Penguin Books)

period, family historians will find many other names in their ancestry that don't appear in the standard reference books. Some may be indications of immigrant ancestry. Others perhaps preserve some long-forgotten incident. The answer may lie in a document somewhere, waiting to be discovered, or it may remain a puzzle for ever.

ABOVE Until recently, women always took their husband's surname on marriage.

Keeping records

Although you may not have much paper to file yet, a lot will soon accumulate, so setting up an efficient filing system is essential. Most people already have or develop individual methods that best suit them and the records they collect.

STARTING A FILING SYSTEM

A good way to start is to get two large ring binders. The first one will include information you are certain of; the second will include notes you have taken that may be relevant but that you cannot yet link to your family. Divide both into one section per family name you are researching. As your research progresses and the paperwork increases, you may need to give a separate ring binder to each name.

You will also need a master copy of your descent. You could draw your own, but they are available by mail order or in the bookshops of record offices and libraries such as the Society of Genealogists. These are daunting but exciting – the one produced by the Church of Jesus Christ of Latter-day Saints (LDS) has space for 12 generations, which potentially includes over 3,000 ancestors.

CHOOSING A SYSTEM OF IDENTIFICATION

Each ancestor must have a unique number. This can be a single figure (usually already printed on the chart) or you might want to assign each generation a number, usually a Roman numeral, starting with yourself as I1, your parents as II1 (your father) and II2 (your mother), and so on. This will tell you straightaway which generation

ABOVE When you copy any information from documents, ensure you note where it came from and the archive's reference number.

you are dealing with, but will present problems for your descendants. You also run into difficulties with marriages between cousins, especially those from different generations, which could make a great-grandparent also a great-great-grandparent.

Most people use a computer programme to record their family history that includes a method of distinguishing generations and individuals. If you are using a printed master chart, each ancestor will be assigned a unique number. Remember to write this number on any documents relating to the individual. Some professional genealogists use letters instead of numerals. One system, devised by the Surname Index in Sussex, gives each 30-year period from 1380 onwards a letter of the alphabet, starting with A (1380–1409) and finishing with Z

(2130–59). The period of 30 years was chosen because that is the average length of a generation. This system presents problems if one of your ancestors had children in two different time periods. Or if an ancestor was born at the beginning of one of these periods and had children young. His or her children would then share the same generation letter.

As you file material related to a particular ancestor, you should annotate it with the ancestor's number (or letter) to prevent confusion between family members with the same name. You might also want to give all the children of an ancestor a reference number. To prevent numbers getting out of hand, you could assign the siblings of an ancestor the same number plus a, b, c, d and so on. Your father's brother (your paternal uncle) would become 2a or II1a.

Alternatively, you might prefer to write "William Smith brother of John Smith 2/II 1" on any notes relating to him.

KEEPING FURTHER RECORDS

In addition to the files containing your research results, you will need a notebook. A hardback book is a good idea because it is sturdier and more difficult to lose than single sheets of paper, but you will have to copy the information in order to file it in the right section of your master research file. A more sensible alternative is a block of paper with ring binder holes punched in it: sheets with errors on can just be torn out and disposed of, and once a sheet is completed it can be filed in a ring binder. You should use a separate sheet of paper for each document or source.

Whether you choose to have a separate book in which you list all the sources you have searched, or whether you record this information at the back of your main notebook, is up to you. Making lists of everything you look at is essential to prevent reading the same document more than once. It is also a good idea to have a small copy

ABOVE **Laptops are a convenient way to store and manipulate your findings.**

Understanding the law

Many countries have legislation covering information that can be stored on computers or in paper files. Check what the position is where you live.

When you copy information, especially from the internet and published books, you also need to be aware of copyright law, especially if you publish your work in an article, a book or even on the internet. This might seem unlikely at the beginning of your search but who knows!

When you copy or print out information, always note the source and perhaps put the words you have quoted in inverted commas as a reminder that they are not your own work and therefore may be subject to copyright law or other legislation, such as privacy.

---

of each separate family tree on an A5 index card in a small ring binder or display book. It needs to give just the dates and places of birth/baptism, marriage and death/burial of each family member (including siblings). It is surprising how often you will be researching one branch of the family when you unexpectedly come across something that could relate to another branch. If you have a basic chart with you, you can refer to it on the spot and open up a whole new avenue of research.

When you get in touch with other people who share your research interests, you will need to decide whether to have a separate file for their correspondence or whether to file their letters with the relevant branch of the family.

USING A COMPUTER

There are a number of excellent software packages for family historians, on which you can prepare charts, store notes and so on, but they are not a total substitute for paper files. This is mainly because even if you back up everything, you still run the risk of losing all your research through computer or memory stick failure. Print out your work regularly so that if there is a problem you will lose comparatively little information. Anything you do

lose should be able to be easily reconstructed from your most recent notes.

You can buy or produce on your computer standard forms to help with your record-keeping. They include:

1. Family sheets, which give details of a marriage and all the children of it, including where they were born/baptized, whom they married and when, and the date of their death/burial. Each sheet is numbered, and at the bottom of the entry for each child there is a space in which to write the number of any further sheets relating to them.

2. Individual sheets, which contain details of an individual's life. As well as birth, baptism and parentage; marriage(s); children; death and burial; there is space for where they were living at particular dates, what they were doing, the dates the will (if any) was written and proved and where this information came from.

FURTHER HELP

Todd, Andrew *Basic Record Keeping for Family Historians* (FHP)
Family History Record Sheets (FHP) contains 21 A4 research record forms including the common research subjects, with a CD containing all the sheets.
Ancestral File: A record book of family research (FHP)

Back to the Early 1800s

By now you should have a basic family tree and some clues that will help you to move back in time. Most of the information you need at this stage is located in the Family Record Centre in London. It holds birth, marriage, adoption and death certificates from 1837 onwards, and records of some of these events overseas.

Certificates after 1837

In 1836 an Act of Parliament was passed to set up the General Register Office (GRO) to record the births, marriages and deaths (BMD) of everyone in England and Wales from 1 July 1837. Before that date, there was no requirement to notify anyone of births and deaths (although churches and other places of worship carried out baptisms and burials). Legal marriages could take place only in Anglican parish churches or be carried out by Jews or the Religious Society of Friends (the Quakers). After 1837, other religious denominations, such as Nonconformists or Roman Catholics, could have their buildings registered to perform marriages.

FINDING BMD CERTIFICATES

Unless you find a complete set of certificates among your family papers, you will need to obtain copies of birth, marriage and (sometimes) death certificates in order to reconstruct your ancestry back to 1837. The GRO has quarterly indexes from the returns sent to them from all over the country. The March quarter covers January, February and March; the June quarter covers April, May and June; the September quarter covers July, August and September; December covers October, November and December. The entries relate to the date of registration, not of the event itself. Certificates can be bought via the GRO's website or from the local register office where the event was registered. You need to copy the name, the registration district, volume no. and page from the indexes for each certificate you order.

The free BMD site (www.freebmd. org.uk) holds indexes to BMD certificates in England and Wales and this is a quick and convenient way to check GRO references to order certificates. Because the information comes from the local register offices, it may be more accurate than the GRO indexes. The commercial genealogical sites usually have digitized copies of the GRO indexes. Some local record offices and libraries have copies of the indexes on microfiche.

Birth certificates

When researching your ancestry, you must start from the known and work back to the unknown. In certificate terms, this means getting the birth certificate of a child in order to find out the parents' names, then using this information to look for the parents' marriage certificate, which will give their fathers' names and occupations. You can then order the birth certificate of each parent, and so find out their mothers' names as well.

In reality, unfortunately, it never goes this smoothly. In the first ten years or so following the introduction of national registration, parents were

ABOVE This birth certificate from 1837 will have been relatively easy to find because it was compiled after the setting up of the General Register Office in 1836.

not obliged to notify the registrar of a child's birth, and if a child was not registered within six months, it could not be included in the records. There seems also to have been some confusion about whether it was necessary to register a child if it had also been baptized. In 1874, fines were introduced for non-notification, which improved the situation. This lack of registration, combined with the bureaucracy involved in copying entries as they were passed from level to level in the system, means that a number of events are missing from the indexes, especially in the earlier period. There may be as many as 15 percent of the births missing for 1837–47, and as many as 1 in 40 marriages missing for 1837–99. There are also difficulties caused by copying errors and by dealing with illiterate people who may not know how their names were written.

Marriage certificates

In the days when divorce was practically impossible for poor people, many just left their spouse and set up another family with someone else, claiming to be married to them. Some did marry after the first spouse's death, but others did not, and their children never knew that they were illegitimate.

If either of the parties had connections with Scotland, Ireland or another country, the marriage may have taken place there. It is also worth checking the miscellaneous indexes that cover events at sea and abroad. One reason for marrying abroad was that the parties were related. All these factors may account for people not appearing in registers where they are expected to be.

Death certificates

It is comparatively easy to find birth and marriage certificates, since most people had children soon after the marriage, but as people can die at any time, finding a death certificate can be a much longer job. It is also common to find that ages at death are approximate, since the informant might not have known the exact date of birth.

SEARCHING THE INDEXES

Researching information in the indexes calls for patience, diligence, concentration and imagination. It is easy to overlook a name at the bottom of a page, especially if you have been searching for a long time. Take regular breaks. Note all the quarters you have checked, as it is easy to take a break and forget which one you were going to look at. This can lead to you looking at the same one twice and missing the one that you need.

Be meticulous

Be careful not to miss the reference. It is easy to overlook a name, especially if you have been searching for a long time and are tired. If you are using the books at the FRC, run a sheet of paper down the names to keep your eyes focused on the right place. This also ensures that you do not miss the last one lurking at the bottom of the page. This task is more difficult if you're using microfiche.

Leave no gaps

As you work, list all the quarters you have checked, both year and month. It is all too easy, if someone is using the next book that you want to consult, to work on another, planning to go back and then either not do so or forget which one you were going to look at. This can lead to you looking at the same one twice and missing the one that you need.

Try alternative spellings

Ask yourself what a surname might have sounded like to the registrar, if the informant had a heavy cold or a speech impediment, for example Searle/Thurle. Names beginning with an H cause particular problems, because dropping the H is common in many

ABOVE After 1837 marriages could take place in a register office rather than a church, but most people still preferred a traditional church wedding.

Significant dates in the history of BMD records

1837 1 July Civil registration began in England and Wales.

1866 Death indexes recorded age at death.

1907 Deceased Wife's Sister Marriage Act permitted a man to marry his deceased wife's sister.

1911 September Birth indexes contained mother's maiden name.

1912 Marriage indexes showed name of the second party.

1921 Deceased Brother's Widow Marriage Act permitted a woman to marry her deceased husband's brother.

1926 Adoption of Children Act provided for adoption of children, with the creation of an Adopted Children's Register.

1926 Legitimacy Act allowed for illegitimate children to be re-registered on the subsequent

marriage of the parents.

1927 Registration of stillbirths made compulsory (but the register was not put on open access).

1929 It became illegal for anyone under 16 to marry. Previously girls could marry at 12 and boys at 14, although they needed their parents' consent until they were 21.

1931 Marriage between uncle and niece/aunt and nephew allowed.

1947 Short birth certificate introduced. (This does not contain parents' names and so is of no use to the genealogist.)

1949 Register of Births and Deaths in Aircraft listed any births or deaths that took place in aircraft registered in Great Britain or Northern Ireland, wherever they occurred in the world.

1959 Legitimacy Act allowed the

children born when one of their parents was married to somebody else to be legitimized when their parents married. The child could be re-registered if it had been previously entered under the woman's husband's name.

1969 Death indexes showed date of birth.

1969 Age of majority reduced from 21 to 18. Parental consent to marriage now needed for people under 18.

1975 Children Act 1975 allowed adopted children to obtain the original information on their birth certificate.

1986 People permitted to marry a stepchild or stepgrandchild, but both parties had to be over 18 and the child must not have been treated as a child of the person's family.

---

local accents, so for Horton try Orton. When handwritten indexes were copied, confusion between M and W could occur, such as Mardell/Wardell. If you look at samples of copperplate handwriting, you will see that confusion between F, J and T was also possible.

Consider alternative first names

Consider whether the person was actually given the name by which he or she was generally known. Children named after a parent might have been known by their second or another name to prevent confusion. Others, for reasons long forgotten, might have been called something completely unrelated to their original name. Alternatively, the parents may not have decided on the child's name until after it was registered.

There was, and still is, no obligation to give a first name, so you need to

check at the top of the list of surnames to see if there is a likely registration in the area where the family lived.

Consider illegitimacy

Illegitimate children were given their mother's surname until 1926, when they could be re-registered with the father's name if the parents married after the birth. Also, a couple might not have married until after some, or all, of their children were born.

Broaden your time span

Ages are often inaccurately recorded, so check up to five years on either side of the likely date. If you are relying on the ages given on a marriage certificate to find the person's birth certificate, consider that the ages have been falsified.

Ages at death are especially suspect because the informant may not have known the age and just made a guess.

Consider other districts

The event would have been registered where it took place, not where the family lived. Women might have gone to stay with their mothers or other family members for the birth of a child, and so the birth would have been registered there. Even a hospital just a short distance from home might have been in another registration district.

Narrow the field

If you are researching a fairly common surname, you may find a number of entries, any of which might be the person you are seeking. The staff at both the FRC and the local record office will do some (paid) cross-checking for you, usually within a limited time frame. You can ask them to check entries until they find a particular piece of information that matches something you know already, such as the father's first name. Alternatively, you could:

1. Order all the possible certificates; but this can be expensive and may not necessarily help you to decide which one is your ancestor.

2. Look for the birth certificate of a brother or sister about whom you know more (such as exact date or place of birth) or who has a rarer first name.

3. Note the quarters and reference details, then seek out other, more distant, family members in the hope that one of them will know something or have a document that will help.

If none of this works, it can mean going back to the original entry and paying for a search to be made in a local register office.

RESEARCHING BMD CERTIFICATES

Consider carefully whether you need your ancestor's birth certificate. You may find that getting a sibling's would be more useful: you will still get the parents' names from it and you might also get the family's address.

In England and Wales, a time given on a birth certificate means twins or a multiple birth, so you need to look for another child or children with the same surname and reference number to find out their names. If you want to know what order they were born in, you will have to order the certificates.

On freebmd you can click on the page number next to a name to see all the names on the same page. This can help with multiple births and also for marriages to find a spouse's surname if you only know the first name. If you know the names of both parties, look up the less common name on freebmd or in the indexes. When using just the indexes, either online or on microfiche, note the reference number against the one you think is your

ancestor, and then look up the other party's name in the same quarter's index. If the reference number is the same, you can be fairly sure that you have the right marriage and you can order the certificate.

Death certificates are not especially useful in constructing family trees. After 1866 the ages at death are given in the indexes, which will give a starting point to look for a birth certificate. If you know that the widow or widower remarried, you can look for their marriage certificate after that date. Using freebmd is a quick way to find out when an ancestor died, whether or not you decide to order a certificate.

Levels of registration
Registrars
At the lowest, local level, the 2,193 registrars recorded births, marriages and deaths. Four times a year they sent a copy of these certificates to the district Superintendant Registrar.

Superintendent Registrars
In 1834, Poor Law Unions (groups of

FURTHER HELP

Annal, David & Collins, Audrey *Birth Marriage and Death Records for Family Historians* (Pen & Sword)
Langston, Brett (compiler) *A Handbook to the Civil Registration Districts of England and Wales* (FHP)
General Register Office website www.gro.gov.uk

parishes) were set up, and they became the basis for the new registration system. Each union had a Superintendent Registrar, who was responsible for a number of local registrars. After checking the entries from the registrars in his district, each Superintendent Registrar sent copies to the General Register office (GRO).

GRO in Somerset House, London
A quarterly index, covering the whole of England and Wales, was drawn up from copies of the certificates sent by the local register offices to Superintendent Registrars.

ABOVE It is interesting to know when, where and how someone died, but the actual information on a death certificate will rarely help you move back in time.

Miscellaneous Events

The National Archives holds papers relating to divorce and some BMD overseas or at sea. You will need a Reader's Ticket to look at the original papers but they are increasingly being put online. Adoption is a special case and there are a number of other BMD events that are not included in the main GRO indexes.

DIVORCES

The original divorce files for England & Wales between 1858–1958 (except for the period 1945–50) are in TNA and are listed in the catalogue by the names of the parties. Divorce case files from 1858-1911 are on the Ancestry website. Before 1858, divorces could be made only through an Act of Parliament. Formal separations and annulments were obtained through the Church courts, so papers relating to them will be in CROs or DROs.

ADOPTIONS

Before 1926, adoptions were arranged informally. After that date, a register of adopted children was set up. The indexes are arranged by the adoptive name, and the certificates do not contain information about birth parents. No information is online. People wishing to obtain an original birth certificate should contact the Adoption Section at the GRO to inquire about the procedures, at www.gov.uk/adoption-records.

EVENTS OVERSEAS

In addition to events in England and Wales, TNA contains copies of a number of records relating to overseas. These came mainly from maritime, military or consular sources. Most are from the 19th century, but some date back to 1627 and some continue until the late 1950s. They are divided between statutory returns (those that had to be made by law) and non-statutory returns (those that were made voluntarily). There are indexes on the TNA website with information about the location of the original documents.

From 1627 onwards, miscellaneous notifications of BMD overseas were returned to Britain. These were largely to ensure that, should any dispute arise, the people concerned could prove that they were married, that their children were legitimate, or that someone was dead. Many are BMD of embassy or other government staff, or those notified to the local consulate by British people either visiting the coun-

ABOVE A photograph in your family album of a merchant seaman, like this one from 1870, may mean BMD records at sea.

try or resident there. These are not limited to British territories, though some of these are included, but cover places in Europe where there were sizeable British communities, and countries elsewhere. From 1849, consuls were allowed to carry out marriages and had to make a return of the ceremonies to the GRO in London. Researchers must pay the standard certificate fee to get copies of the information from the statutory returns. The originals have been scanned and indexed and are available at www.bmdregisters.co.uk.

ARMY BMD

Regimental registers were kept from 1761 and are most likely to contain births in depots in Great Britain. In addition, army regiments each had their own chaplain, who generally kept a register of the christenings, marriages and burials (CMB) he carried out. Chaplains' returns from 1796 are most likely to contain births overseas. Indexes are online at TNA, and documents are on findmypast.

BMD AT SEA

From 1837, BMD at sea on British ships had to be notified to the GRO. By an Act of 1874, which did not affect the Royal Navy, certificates of births and deaths on Merchant Navy ships and passenger ships travelling to and from British ports had to be sent to the Register General of Shipping and Seamen. From here, they were distributed to the Register Offices in London, Edinburgh and Dublin, depending on the nationality of the people involved (though this wasn't always strictly observed). Certificates concerning foreigners went to the London office. There is a TNA factsheet about the various sources that can be accessed online from commercial sites. They contain only births and deaths. There are indexes to deaths in the armed forces during and just after the Boer War (1899–1902), World War I (1914–21) and World War II (1939–48). Deaths at sea during the two World Wars were sometimes sent to the GRO but were mainly passed to the Admiralty, which maintained a separate register, so consult both.

THE MISCELLANEOUS INDEXES

If you have to visit the FRC and a member of your family spent time abroad, it may be worthwhile checking out the various miscellaneous indexes.

The information in the miscellaneous returns may be found elsewhere, such as the records of the Bishop of London, which are in LMA, or the Oriental and India Office Library, which is at the British Library. If you find that the information you want is recorded on a certificate for which a fee is payable, you can save the money by exploring these alternative sources. This is definitely worth considering if you know you will be doing other research in that particular archive.

Maritime war deaths (1794–1964) are on findmypast but there are also some indexed files from the Admiralty that can be seen at TNA. Seamen who died in the course of a voyage had their

wages and effects given to the next of kin or someone nominated in their will. Records relating to this are at TNA, so if you know that your ancestor was a seaman, you might prefer to go to TNA rather than the FRC.

Children born at sea were sometimes given the name of the ship on which they were born, so if you trace an ancestor with an odd name that appears to have no family connections, this may be a clue to their birthplace.

ABOVE Deaths of Army personnel who died overseas in wartime are indexed. Sailors' deaths are more likely to be in Admiralty records at TNA than with GRO certificates.

LEFT As a resident in France at the time of his death in 1900, Oscar Wilde's death certificate is in the Miscellaneous Foreign Deaths returns.

FURTHER HELP

Stafford, Georgina *Where to Find Adoption Records: A guide for counsellors, adopted people and birth parents* (British Agencies for Adoption and Fostering)

Censuses

Following some local head counts held at irregular intervals, the nationwide censuses held from 1841 give the family historian a snapshot of the life of their ancestors at ten-yearly intervals. Digitized and indexed copies are available on the internet from the commercial websites or from FreeCen. Digitized copies up to 1891 are available on CD-Rom, film or microfiche, local record offices may have copies but will only have indexes if these have been done by local or family history societies. Some societies have published their indexes on CD-Rom.

The first censuses

Although not official censuses, there have been head counts of people since the Domesday survey in 1086. Various towns and parishes, such as Poole, Dorset, in 1575 and Ealing in 1522, listed everyone living there, and since those dates many other censuses have been made. Some of them named only the head of the household and added how many people there were in it.

National censuses were first proposed in 1753, but it wasn't until 1800 that legislation to enumerate the entire population of England and Wales was passed. The first census was held on Monday, 10 March 1801, and was carried out by parish officials in England and Wales and schoolmasters in Scotland. Thereafter, a national census was taken every ten years. The next three – in 1811, 1821 and 1831 – were also taken by the same people, but in 1841 the government took over. Only some copies of the first four censuses survive in parish records, but from 1841 there is full coverage of the whole country.

ABOVE Until the last century, a whole family might live in one room, so several, unrelated households may be found in the same house.

BELOW These gypsies have had their census papers brought to them by the police, but many gypsies and other travellers, as well as the homeless sleeping rough, were not recorded in the earlier census returns.

The 1841 census

From 1841, it was decided to seek information about everyone in each house on a particular night (in this case, 6–7 June). The information gathered was broadly similar to previous ones, with the significant addition of the age of each person. Exact ages were required only for children under 16; adults' ages were rounded down to the nearest five years. Thus a person stated to be 30 could have been any age between 30 and 34. People were also required to say whether or not each person had been born in the same county in which they now lived and whether any member of the household was foreign-born. There are, however, omissions from this census: miners on shift were not included, for example, and nor were people on board ships that were in harbour.

The 1851 census

There were several changes in the questions that were asked for this census, which was held on the night of

30–1 March. Instead of asking how many actual houses there were, the government now wanted to know the number of households. More than one household might live in a house, particularly in poor areas, where whole families might live in one room. A line was drawn across the page under each household.

People were also required to state the parish in which they were born. This is what makes this census so useful to the family historian. Those born overseas, however, were required to put only the country, although some did include the place within it. Others put "British citizen", which suggests one of three options: that they were naturalized, had denization or were born in a British colony. For this census, sailors on ships in harbour were included but not, it appears, people on canal barges.

A question about whether a person was deaf, dumb, blind or lunatic was also asked, although it was not until the 1881 census that the kind of disability was specified. If everyone is ticked this is more likely to be marks that were made when the numbers were being added up.

Censuses for 1861 and 1871

Held on the nights of 7–8 April and 2–3 April respectively, these asked the same questions as the 1851 census.

The 1881 census

This census, which was held on the night of 3–4 April, was indexed in a project carried out by the Federation of Family History Societies (FFHS) and the Church of Jesus Christ of Latter-day Saints (LDS). This index exists on both microfiche and CD-ROM and can also be accessed for free on Familysearch and other websites.

A separate note of whether an individual was lunatic, imbecile or idiot was made, replacing the "lunatic" option in earlier censuses.

ABOVE Neath Place, London (c.1900), no longer exists. Maps from the 19th century will be needed to find out where it was.

RIGHT A 19th-century census map showing the districts of Epping, Chigwell and Harlow, in Essex.

The 1891, 1891 and 1901 censuses

These censuses were held on the night of 5–6 April, 31 March–1 April and 5–6 April respectively and requested the same information as the census of 1881.

The 1911 census

This census was held on the night of 2–3 April. It is the first for which the original forms, filled in by the householders themselves, have survived so the family historian can see their ancestor's handwriting. New questions were asked about how long a marriage had lasted, the total number of children born and how many were still alive. More details about occupations were required and, as well as asking for a person's place of birth, nationality was also entered.

RESEARCHING THE CENSUSES

You need to have an idea of where your ancestor was living at the time of a particular census. This information can come from various sources, such as BMD certificates, trade directories, such as Kelly's, and private correspondence. This will help to narrow down the possibilities when using the indexes, especially if your ancestor had a common name.

Using a combination of name, likely age, birthplace or residence and adding keywords, such as occupations, will also help to pinpoint individuals but remember there may be errors. Most of the indexing (apart from the 1881) of the online censuses was done overseas so those inputting the data would not necessarily have had the knowledge of likely spellings of surnames and place names to help them decipher difficult handwriting. You can see if a previous researcher has queried something, and you can add corrections yourself. And of course, the information originally given might not be entirely accurate.

If you check the Advanced Search options on the websites, this may give further details to fill in. Most have the option to include a relative: spouse, father, mother or sibling. It is, however, better not to put in too many.

In most search engines you have the option of using wildcards, substituting a symbol like * for a letter or letters. This means that if you are searching for a name like Kates and you put in Ka*es, you will also get Kales and

ABOVE Censuses were originally carried out to find statistical information about the population.

RIGHT Trade directories, such as Kelly's, can help you find the address of an individual's workplace, which may help you trace them in the relevant census.

Kafes, which are possible spelling or transcription errors.

Alternatively, if you can't find your ancestor where you expect him or her to be, consider other options, like a boarding school or university, the workhouse, hospital or even prison. Check these places by putting 'school', 'university', 'workhouse', 'hospital', 'asylum', 'prison' or 'gaol'/'jail', etc, into the keyword box. People in mental hospitals and gaols were usually only listed by their initials, so you may find it useful to search by initials, plus birthplace, age, occupation, etc. You can also try 'visitor' to see if they were paying a visit to friends or family on the night of the census. It's also a good idea to check the local area. Most people had relatives nearby.

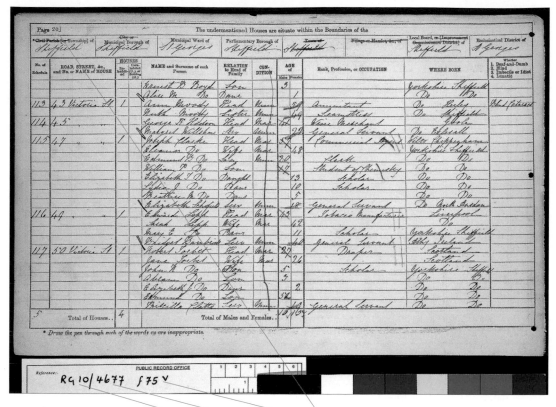

ABOVE A page from the 1871 census. class mark   piece number   folio number   page number

Sometimes you may need to make your way through an entire area. You can check out whole streets or villages on the online censuses. Some County Record Offices and local studies libraries have copies for their area on film, and many have been indexed by family history societies. Check whether this has been done for the area you are interested in to save yourself a considerable amount of work.

As England's capital city, London is a special case because many inhabitants were highly mobile. You may also find that many people have the same name, even if it is a comparatively rare one. Local and family historians working on it have created a number of indexes and lists of inhabitants.

To find out where your London-based family was living in a census year, it is sometimes better to get the birth certificate of a sibling born in the year of the census rather than the ancestor, as this will give you an address. This is where death certificates can be useful, as it might also give the address at which a family was living. You won't know whether the person died at home or in hospital until you've paid for the certificate.

Although marriage certificates give addresses for both bride and groom, you should not rely on this. For a small fee, couples would leave a suitcase somewhere, usually a lodging house in the parish where they planned to marry, and claim to be resident there, thus

saving money by having the banns called in one place rather than in two.

Once you have found out where those ancestors who lived before the advent of civil registration in 1837 were born, go to the parish records. J35

Chapman, Colin R. *Pre-1941 Census and Population Listings in the British Isles* (Lochin Pub.)

Christian, Peter & Annal, David *Census: the expert guide* (TNA)

Gibson, Jeremy & Medlycott, Mervyn *Local Census Listings 1522-1930 Holdings in the British Isles* (FHP)

Raymond, Stuart A., *The Census 1801-1911: A Guide for the Internet Era* (FHP)

The International Genealogical Index and other indexes

At this stage, you may have enough information to start linking you and your family to information that is already available and to other people researching the same names. Even if you haven't, this is a section to revisit regularly as your research advances – there's no point in laboriously repeating work that someone else has already done. The growth of interest in genealogy has led to the gathering and dissemination of a huge amount of data. It may not be much use to you at this stage in your research, but the sources are described here to encourage you and to reassure you that soon they can be used to reduce the time-consuming record-searching.

ABOVE One of the granite vaults in Utah where the Church of Jesus Christ of Latter-day Saints stores records and copies of archive material from around the world.

THE INTERNATIONAL GENEALOGICAL INDEX

The International Genealogical Index (IGI) was set up by the LDS. The Mormons believe that, in order to be reunited with their ancestors in the next world, forebears must be retrospectively baptized into their Church. They have a massive programme of entering data on baptisms and marriages. The majority of entries for the United Kingdom are pre-1837 and come from parish and other Church registers. This enormous database has been placed on the Internet but is also available on CD-ROM, and on microfiche held in record offices and libraries. The IGI is most helpful once you get back before the mid-19th century and civil registration.

Names are arranged by county, with all spelling variants listed together. Within each surname, the entries are put in alphabetical order of first and then subsequent names. Baptisms and marriages are itemized; there are very few burials included.

In some ways the microfiche version of the records is the most useful for the genealogist, since it is easy to get a photocopy from which information can be quickly extracted. You can highlight all the entries before or after a particular date, in a particular place, or all the children of a particular marriage. This is possible, but more laborious, on printouts from the CD-ROM and Internet versions, and the results are less easy to take in since they do not form a coherent visual pattern.

When using the IGI, there are a number of points to bear in mind. First, its purpose is not primarily for family history: it has been compiled

ABOVE Records are ent from Utah to local Family History Centers around the world.

ABOVE The entrance to the LDS vaults, housed within a granite mountain.

for religious reasons, so it does not contain all the information a family historian needs.

Second, there are, inevitably, errors in the data (though this is true of almost all indexes). You must always check the original record, where you may also find additional information. The IGI does not, for example, say whether people getting married were single or widow(er)s of the parish they came from, as opposed to the one where they married. This sort of information will, however, be included in the original record.

Third, although you can, in many cases, compile a rough family tree from the entries on the IGI, not all registers and all dates have been entered. You cannot therefore assume that the John and Mary Smith in a certain village in 1800 are necessarily the ancestors of a John Smith in the same village in 1900. You will need to use other documents before you are able to prove a link.

Finally, the IGI does not include burials, though the word "child" indicates that the person died before the age of eight. This has not been recorded consistently, however, so you cannot always be sure to which entries an early death applies.

The IGI is a finding aid, not a comprehensive record that can be used by itself. With all these reservations, however, it must be said that the IGI is one of the most useful tools a family historian has, so it is worth spending time learning how to use it.

FAMILY TREE

As well as the IGI, extracted from parish registers, other sources are all being brought together on the Family-Search site, combined into one indexed database. All the records for each individual go into one folder, and

ABOVE Using a microfiche reader to search the IGI for family history data.

each folder is linked to a pedigree, where possible. This has become the Family Tree section, which includes family trees created by members of the LDS Church. You can still consult the IGI online by using the Search tab.

OTHER INDEXES

There are many other, smaller indexes compiled by Family History Societies and individuals. Some relate to occupations, some are of marriages in a particular area, of criminal records, of inquests, of apprenticeships and so on. The indexes can be recorded on paper, microfiche, microfilm or CD-ROM. Many CROs have copies relating to their areas, and the Society of Genealogists (SoG) library has copies of most of them.

RIGHT GOONS has a website and also publishes material.

FURTHER HELP

Gibson, Jeremy and Hampson, Elizabeth *Specialist Indexes for Family Historians* (FHP)

THE GUILD OF ONE-NAME STUDIES

Acting as an umbrella group of individual societies, the Guild of One-Name Studies (GOONS) consists of members who have an interest in a particular surname. The names vary from the relatively common to the extremely rare.

If you have an unusual name in your ancestry, it is worth getting their directory or logging on to their website (www.one-name.org) to see if one of their members has the same interest as you. Some genealogists also advertise the names they are researching in family history magazines. By getting in touch with them you might save yourself some time-consuming research.

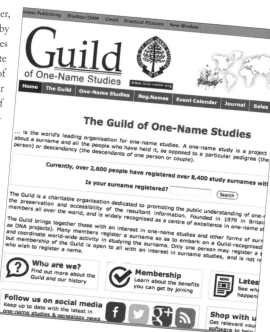

Using the internet

Although, in some ways, the internet has made researching family history much easier, the hype around it has raised expectations to an unreasonable level. It is, however, now an essential tool. Original records are increasingly being digitized and made accessible online, but not everything is yet there. Research in archives or libraries is still essential. What the internet can do is help to locate original documents quickly and conveniently. Catalogues of CROs and libraries on their website help to plan research and many record offices, libraries and museums have online fact sheets that can be studied at home.

The websites of organizations of all kinds usually provide a brief history, which will help family historians understand what may be available from its archives and where these are now located. They also give valuable background information that will further your understanding of the lives of your ancestors.

SEARCH ENGINES

A search engine is a way of finding every website that contains the word or words that you enter. It is generally agreed that Google is the best search engine, because it arranges the results in order of how frequently they are consulted, but there are others. They are particularly useful for finding websites on a specific subject, but if you enter just a personal name you will get every site on the web containing that name. Putting in a common name, such as Johnson, or an ancestor who shares a name with someone famous, such as Elizabeth Taylor, will produce

ABOVE **The internet offers a world of information and allows easy communication with family historians around the globe**.

too many irrelevant results. If you put words in quotation marks, like "family history" you will get that exact phrase. You can try adding dates, places and occupations. If you put plus sign (+) before a word, only those websites that include the word will come up. Put a minus sign (–) before a word, like –film –star, and the results will exclude websites accordingly.

It is worth trying searches using two or three search engines. Sometimes, however, you have to accept that the information you need has simply not been researched or put on the web. In addition to extracting information from the websites of various organizations and individuals (which can also contain family histories), there are often links that provide ways of communicating with other researchers.

EMAIL

This is the most obvious way of writing to someone who shares the same interests as you. Most individuals who have a website on which, for example, they have placed information about their family history will list an email address, which can be used to communicate directly with that person.

MAILING LISTS

All subscribers receive a copy of every communication sent via email. For some of the larger and more general lists, this can be as many as fifty a day, so consider carefully which mailing list or lists you will find most useful. They have specialist interests: a geographical area; an occupation or group of occupations; ancestors from overseas, etc. The lists are managed by a server, but subscription is generally free.

NEWSGROUPS AND MESSAGE BOARDS

These are the electronic equivalent of a notice board and are also dedicated to particular topics. Search engines, such as Google and Yahoo, and genealogical sites, such as RootsWeb, host groups where people sharing the same interests can exchange information. People can simply post messages, asking for information, recommending (or warning against) professional researchers or websites, or writing about a specialist topic.

Messages on these sites are not automatically sent to subscribers, so they need to be checked regularly to make sure something of interest is not missed. These sites will also probably have archives of material that has

Using the internet wisely

- You may need specific software to access certain types of information on the internet. This can often be downloaded from an internet site, but you should get advice about what is necessary if you are not a confident computer user.
- Be focused: it is very easy to spend a long (and potentially expensive) time going through a lot of unrelated records. Formulate questions and strategies for answering them before you start.
- Regard the internet as a giant index. Like all other indexes, it is basically a guide to original documents.
- Treat information on it with caution: anyone can set up their own internet site and put whatever they like on it. A great deal of supposition might be presented as fact. Ask

yourself: how authoritative is this source?
- Be wary about handing over money on the internet. The reputable genealogical sites, which charge for access to their databases and archives, are reliable and generally safe, but buying objects, such as coats of arms, from sites based overseas can be problematic. You have little redress if the goods are not delivered, and giving credit card details on the internet can present problems of security.
- You will find sites offering books that claim to list all of the people with the same surname as you. These are not researched genealogical publications, but are simply lists of usually unrelated people compiled from readily available sources, such as telephone directories. Ignore them.

FURTHER HELP

Christian, Peter *The Genealogist's Internet* (TNA)
Morris, Heather *Researching Your Family History Online* (Pearson Education) a good resource for absolute beginners
Local libraries often run courses on using the internet

PUBLISHING ON THE INTERNET

As well as using the internet to find and communicate with people with the same research interests, you should consider putting your own family tree and history on the web, so that you can be contacted by others.

You could also create your own website but you may need professional help or a course to do this. Investigate some existing sites to get an idea of how best to do it. Look at the sites you find easiest to use and let them guide you in organizing your own genealogical information.

previously appeared, and it is a good idea to check these out.

NETIQUETTE AND FREQUENTLY ASKED QUESTIONS (FAQS)

There are conventions about communicating on the internet, and if you break the rules you may be excluded from group communication sites. Most will, however, have a list of procedures they expect their members to observe. When first starting out it is helpful to remember that people on well established sites can get irritated by beginners posing the same basic questions. To avoid this happening, most sites have a list of Frequently Asked Questions (FAQs) that you should consult to see whether your query has already been answered.

ABOVE The IGI is easily accessible to family historians through the LDS website.

Genealogical sites

The following sites contain information, advice and links for family historians. The information on these sites is constantly being supplemented, so they are worth checking regularly to see what is new. The commercial sites often offer some material free for a limited time, then charge a fee.

Family search
www.familysearch.org
This is the free online database of the LDS. It is increasingly being used to publish family histories but it also contains the International Genealogical Index (IGI); records of events, mainly baptisms and marriages, from all over the world. The IGI is also available in some libraries on microfiche or CD-Rom. These references have mainly been created from filmed copies of parish registers. Not all have yet been transcribed. The library catalogue can identify which copies of records it holds, and for a fee you can request film copies for viewing to be sent to your local LDS Family History Center.

RootsWeb
www.rootsweb.ancestry.com
A free, American-based site with links to other sites, this also hosts message boards, mailing lists and newsgroups. There are a number of volunteer projects providing indexes to various types of documents and records around the world.

Genuki www.genuki.org.uk
This free site is a portal maintained by volunteers. It contains links to all the CROs in the UK and Ireland, to Family History Societies and one-name groups.

Cyndi's List www.cyndislist.com
A free, American-based portal with worldwide links, particularly strong on advice about tracing American ancestry. It also contains advice about publishing on the internet.

ABOVE RootsWeb was one of the oldest sites for family historians. It hosts volunteer projects to put information on the web.

ABOVE The Origins site is devoted to British genealogical material from England, Scotland and Ireland.

As well as the various free sites, there are commercial sites, either subscription or pay-per-view. The three major commercial sites are currently Ancestry, Findmypast and The Genealogist. They have a lot of material in common, such as the censuses, but each has its own unique sources. Before deciding which to subscribe to and what level of subscription, investigate carefully what their various strengths and weaknesses are. Many local libraries have free access to one of them so check out what is available where you live. Material is added to these sites monthly.

Ancestry www.ancestry.co.uk
This is an American-owned site with branches in different countries. The British branch of the site holds some TNA documents.

Findmypast
www.findmypast.co.uk
This is the major British website for family historians. It has a lot of material from TNA and other English and Welsh repositories.

The Genealogist
www.thegenealogist.co.uk
This is run by S&N Genealogy Supplies, which publishes a lot of genealogical material. This firm also runs www.bmdregisters.co.uk, which has non-parochial registers and www.bmdindexes.co.uk, which has the GRO indexes.

Origins www.origins.net
This contains online British databases, divided into English, Scottish and Irish sections. The major holdings of the three sites are: English Origins www.englishorigins.com has indexes from the SoG, including marriage, licences, apprenticeship records and PCC wills for the period 1750–1800. Scottish Origins www.scotsorigins.com has parish registers, census returns and wills. Irish Origins www.irishorigins.com has census data, Griffith's Valuations, ships' passenger lists and church records.

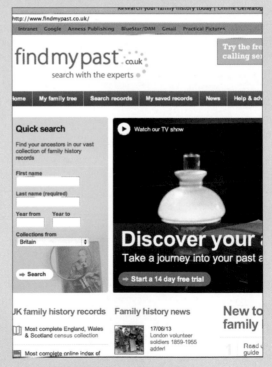

TOP Genuki has links to genealogical organizations in the UK.
ABOVE Ancestry has copies of material from around the world.

ABOVE Findmypast is usually the first online resource that new family historians go to, and is an excellent starting point.

Published material

Not everything is on the internet. Books are still also useful to find out how to research a person, how to interpret primary sources and where to go from there. The following organizations produce books and booklets on aspects of genealogical records that will help you to find answers to your questions and suggest ways to research information that are not immediately obvious. In addition, there are publishers specializing in books of interest to the family and local historian.

THE NATIONAL ARCHIVES

Previously the Public Records Office (PRO), the National Archives (TNA), is the repository for records produced

ABOVE The National Archives is based at Kew, Surrey. TNA, formerly the Public Records Office, it produces many useful books and leaflets about the vast number of records it holds.

ABOVE The SoG site contains details of its holdings, activities and publications.

by the government. It publishes books and research guides on a variety of subjects, concentrating on the different types of records it holds. Its website contains both the catalogue of its records and leaflets on topics of genealogical research, including its holdings in that area. Its books and factsheets on the various branches of the armed services are particularly useful.

THE SOCIETY OF GENEALOGISTS

The SoG has an extensive library of rare books, transcripts of parish registers and documents, archives of family papers and original research, a series of indexes, a book-ordering service and other facilities for the family historian. It also produces a magazine, the Genealogist's Magazine, and booklets on topics of interest

to the family historian. Its series My Ancestor Was... is particularly useful. The library catalogue is included on its website, which also has leaflets about aspects of genealogical research. Nonmembers of the society can use the library on payment of a fee.

THE FAMILY HISTORY PARTNERSHIP

The publication wing of the Federation of Family History Societies has now been closed down. Many of its introductory series of booklets on aspects of genealogical research are now being published in revised editions by the Family History Partnership. It is still worth joining your local family history society because they hold monthly meetings, usually with a lecture on a specialist topic, and most have a computer section where you can get and swap advice. Groups of members often carry out projects to index or reproduce records, which are then published.

The Family History Partnership (FHP) now publishes various Gibson Guides. Jeremy Gibson has produced a number of booklets (sometimes with a co-editor) which detail, county by county, the holdings of record offices on specific subjects, such as coroners' records, poll books, local newspapers, etc. They enable researchers to plan their work in advance by checking whether a record office holds the documents they need to consult. The introductions also give an overview of the records and the kind of information they contain.

PUBLICATIONS

When you are starting out, it is worth subscribing to one or more of the magazines aimed at genealogists. They usually consist of articles on how to research a particular aspect of family history, personal accounts of how a genealogical problem was solved, plus topics of general interest, which build up into a useful body of knowledge. They are especially useful for information on aspects of research that might be too rarely encountered to be included in any of the standard books on genealogy, but which are just what you need to solve a problem.

Specialist publishers

Many companies produce books on genealogy and family history. Pen & Sword, originally primarily a publisher of military history books, has now set up a genealogical section. The Tracing Your... Ancestors series covers specialist areas, like Jewish or Huguenot ancestry, and also regional research, like East Anglia or the North.

The History Press is another specialist publisher of local, family and social history. Since the 19th century

the Harleian Society has been publishing transcripts of registers and pedigrees produced as the result of visitations. Although many of the entries in these transcripts have been entered on the IGI, not all are there, and burials have been excluded from it. The British Record Society also publishes original records. When an interest in genealogy first began in the 19th century, a number of local societies produced transcripts of registers in their area; most County Record Offices have copies of the ones in their counties, and the SoG has a large collection. Many of the earlier books have now been digitized and are available on CD-Rom.

Using published books and records

Before going to original records, check if what you plan to look at has been published. In many cases the records are simply transcripts, though in some cases they may have been translated from Latin, but it will save you having to decipher difficult handwriting.

The majority of published registers and records have already been indexed,

FURTHER HELP

British Record Society:
www.britishrecordsociety.org.uk
The Family History Partnership:
www.thefamilyhistorypartnership
.com
Harleian Society:
www.harleian.org.uk
The History Press:
www.thehistorypress.co.uk
Pen & Sword: www.pen-and-sword.co.uk
Society of Genealogists:
www.sog.org.uk

making them simpler to search than the original documents.

Do not buy books unless it is the only way you can obtain them. It is always preferable to consult them in a library (or borrow them if you can) before deciding how often you will need to use them. The same is true of indexes: if you only need to look up one person on a CD-ROM, weigh the cost of purchase against that of travel to a CRO or specialist library. Also, check to see if the publication you wish to research is already published on the internet.

ABOVE If the document you want to see has been published, you may be able to save time and money by getting it through a library, rather than going to a CRO.

Wills, administrations and death duties

It is often said that you can't take it with you, and wills were made to ensure that a person's possessions went to particular individuals after death. If anybody died intestate (without leaving a will), someone had to be appointed to administer the estate. These administrations (or admons) contain much less information than a will and were usually granted to the next of kin.

WILLS

Most people are familiar with the phrase "last will and testament", which shows the distinction made between land, which cannot be moved, and other goods, which can. The will covers the disposal of estates and property; the testament deals with movable goods, chattels and money.

A history of wills

Until 1858, when a national system was introduced, probate was mainly administered by church courts, but "peculiars" and some manors also had the right to prove wills. During the Commonwealth period (1653–60) a government court handled them.

Nuncupative wills

Before 1838, when nuncupative wills became illegal, a statement of how a person wanted to dispose of his or her possessions could be accepted. They were usually dictated when the person was dying and there wasn't enough time to call in a lawyer or someone experienced in writing a proper will. Although it was witnessed, it was not signed. Such wills usually start with "Memorandum", rather than stating that this is a last will and testament, and are found with the other wills of the court in which they were proved.

Wills before 1858

Before 1858 the proving of wills was done by church courts, which all charged for this service. It has been estimated that in the 19th century only 5 per cent of people's estates went through probate, so the family historian must be prepared not to find a will. When they do exist, however, they can supply a great deal of information.

Wills after 1858

After 1858 the authenticity and validity of wills were proved by the state system on a national basis. The will was taken to the local probate office, which made its own copy and then sent another to the Principal Probate Registry in London, now called the Probate Service of the Principal Registry Family Division. In addition to being the

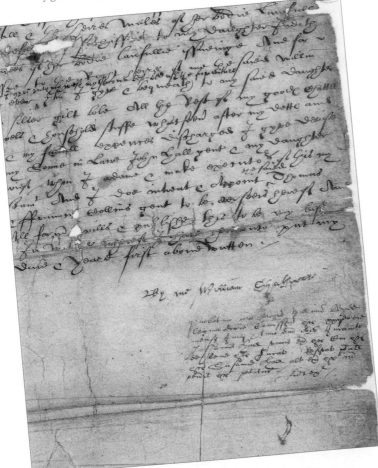

ABOVE Shakespeare's will was fairly simple but provides information about family relationships.

probate office for the south-east of Britain, it also deals with wills that present problems from everywhere in the country, and so is a national centre too. The original will was given back to the executor(s) after a note that probate had been granted was added to it. This conferred on the executor(s) the power to administer the estate.

Locating wills

When trying to find a will before 1858, decide how much property was likely to be left, as this should suggest which level of court to start with, but don't assume that a poor person's will would not have been proved in the Prerogative Court of Canterbury (PCC). Check all the courts (see below).

For 1796–1858 the death duty indexes may be a faster way of finding a will than working your way through the various local probate courts. These indexes cover all courts before 1811, and after that date each court has its own index. They are especially time-saving if you don't know the exact date on which a will was proved. There is a factsheet about how to use them on the TNA site.

Some East India Company (EIC) wills are kept in the Oriental and India Office Library, so those with ancestors living in India, the Far East and other places under the EIC's authority before 1858 might find their wills here.

The national Probate Calendar 1858–1966 is on Ancestry, although the wills themselves are held by the Probate Service. Copies can be obtained by post or a personal search.

If you don't find a will in the area you expect, ask yourself if your ancestor might have died in a "peculiar" (a parish that, for historic reasons, came under the authority of another bishopric or body from the one in which it was geographically located).

ABOVE The reading of a will might cause dissatisfied family members to challenge its contents through one of the courts that dealt with probate.

Probate could take many years to prove, especially if there were any difficulties with the will, if it was challenged by the family or if the person lived overseas. In the days before air travel, it could take many months, even years, before the executor(s) might be able to travel to England to prove the will.

If your ancestor was a soldier or sailor, check TNA first. Soldiers and sailors were encouraged to make wills, especially in times of war.

Find as many wills as you can for all members of your family, not just your direct ancestors. Married men usually left simple wills, dividing their property between their wives and children. More information may come from the wills of single or childless relations, since they tend to distribute possessions among a greater number of relatives, and state the relationship. Maiden aunts are a particularly good source of genealogical information. They may not necessarily have been rich, but they did like to specify just who would receive a particular piece of jewellery or small sum of money.

If a will isn't listed, see if there is a separate list of administrations. (Sometimes the two are given together; sometimes they are in separate registers.)

The courts you will need to check for wills are listed below.

The archdeaconry courts

These courts were the lowest in the hierarchy and were used by people with property in one archdeaconry. These wills are usually in the CRO but may be in a Diocesan Record Office (DRO).

The diocesan courts

Also called consistory or commissary courts, these came under the jurisdiction of a bishop and were used by people who had property in more than one archdeaconry. These wills are usually in the CRO but may be in a DRO.

The Prerogative Court of York (PCY)

The PCY had jurisdiction north of the River Trent. It covered the dioceses of York, Carlisle, Chester, Durham and the Isle of Man, and wills of people who had property in more than one of these dioceses would have been proved here. These wills are in the Borthwick Institute in York and online.

ABOVE The funeral of the Marquis of Bath in 1869. How many of the hundreds of people gathered here were remembered in his will?

someone or some entity other than a court. This might be a manor, a university, the dean and chapter of a cathedral, or the bishop or archdeacon of another diocese.

A sailor's will might be proved in the court connected to the place where he lived in England or Wales; in the archdeaconry or diocesan court of the port in which his ship docked after his death; in the PCC if he died at sea, or in the High Court of the Admiralty.

Of course, wills sometimes created strife in the family, and might have been contested. Any action of this kind will be found in the courts attached to the jurisdiction where they were proved.

Researching wills

To be legal, a will must include one or more executors or executrices (the feminine form of executors). It must also be dated and the signature witnessed by two or more people who must not benefit from the will. If someone dies intestate (without leaving a will), the next of kin can ask for Letters of Administration to be granted so that they can deal with the deceased person's property. These are

The Prerogative Court of Canterbury (PCC)
The PCC was the highest court to prove wills in England and Wales. It was used by those who had property in more than one diocese south of the Trent, or with property in both the PCY and PCC jurisdictions. There was a misapprehension that money invested in the Bank of England counted as property. The bank was sited in the diocese of London, so people who lived elsewhere and had money invested in the bank had their wills proved in the PCC, because they believed that they had property in two dioceses.

The PCC also covered British subjects living abroad in the colonies (including America before the War of Independence, which finished in 1783). During the Commonwealth period (1642–60), all wills were proved in the PCC. These wills are are now available on the TNA website, and can be downloaded for a fee.

All the courts were subject to inhibition from the senior courts. This means that if a bishop were making a

visitation to an archdeaconry, the archdeaconry courts would not be able to carry out their functions, including proving wills. So during the time of the visitation (which usually lasted for a few months), wills would be proved by the diocesan courts.

In addition to these courts, there were "peculiars" (see previous page), which came under the jurisdiction of

---

Digest of will of Sarah Deschamps

TNA PROB 11/995/87
Sarah Deschamps of Maiden Lane, St Paul Covent Garden, widow of Peter Deschamps

To be buried with late husband at Marylebone

To John Deschamps eldest son of my late husband £10

To Francis Deschamps younger son of my late husband £10

To Mrs Susanna Montelln wife of Mr Joseph Montelln

and the daughter of my late husband £10 and my wearing apparel

Remainder to my worthy and most esteemed friend and executrix Mrs Mary Bonouvrier of Maiden Lane

(signed) 15 July 1767

wit: Sam Coates

Mary Hawkes

Proved PCC 12 March 1774

abbreviated to "admon" in records. Also, if the will has not been properly drawn up, for example it was not dated, the next of kin can apply to administer it.

It was, and is still, not necessary to rewrite an entire will in order to vary slightly the bequests within it. The addition of one or more codicils to the will of a member of your family is an interesting source of information about who came into, or fell out of, favour over time.

An inventory – a list of the movable goods of a person – is sometimes attached to a will. This gives clues as to how rich he or she was and also, in the case of men, what their occupation was, since it usually includes his tools.

Be aware that the word "cousin" was used in a much wider sense in the past than it is today. "My cousin Elizabeth" was not necessarily the daughter of an uncle or aunt: she might have been a much more distant relative. All you can tell without further research is that a cousin was a relation of some kind.

If you see that one person, often the eldest son, has been given only a token sum, usually a shilling, don't assume that this is evidence of trouble in the family. He might have already been given a sum of money on marriage or have taken over the family business. Mentioning the person in the will simply showed that he (or occasionally she) had not been forgotten, and so the will could not be challenged on those grounds.

Making a digest of a will

Wills tend to be long and are couched in complicated legal terms, and it is time-consuming and confusing to keep re-reading them to find information. You do need a complete copy of the document for your records, but a digest (a brief summary, in note form,

of the contents) is ideal and convenient for everyday use.

Put where the will comes from, with any reference number given to it by the repository. Enter the person's name, occupation and residence, as given in the document. You can omit the standard opening, but note down any special instructions about funeral arrangements, and so on. Then list all the legatees, their relationship to the testator, what they received and any special conditions attached to the bequest. Also note the name(s) of the executor(s) and whether the testator actually signed the will or simply made a mark (which shows how literate he or she was). Write the date the will was written and the witnesses' names. Add the details of when and where it was proved.

ADMINISTRATION

When a will was found to be valid and proved in court, the executor(s) had to sign a bond for a sum of money that would be forfeited if they did not carry out their duties of administering the estate according to the testator's final wishes, as expressed in the will.

If the deceased person had children who were under the age of majority, it was also the executor(s) job to arrange for their ongoing and future education and welfare by entering into tuition and curation bonds, which were pledges to pay a sum of money if these arrangements were not satisfactory. How this was to be done, including the name of any guardian, may have been stipulated in the will. The bonds that were associated with these various duties should be with the other probate records.

Incomplete or non-existent wills required Letters of Administration to be issued before the estate could be administered.

FURTHER HELP

Probate Search Room, Probate Service, Principal Registry Family Division, First Avenue House, 42–49 High Holborn, London WC1V 6NP
TNA has a fact sheet about finding wills
Grannum, Karen & Taylor, Nigel *Wills & Probate Records: a guide for family historians* (TNA) includes sections on wills in Scotland, Ireland, the Channel Islands and the Isle of Man, as well as in England and Wales.
Raymond, Stuart *Words from Wills and other probate records: a glossary* (FHP)

Some places, such as London, had the right to administer the goods of the orphans of freemen through special courts. These records are separate from the probate courts.

DEATH DUTIES

From 1796, various taxes, called collectively "death duties", were payable on estates worth over a certain amount. Initially the minimum amount was set quite high, so only the largest estates were liable to pay death duties, but during the 19th century it was progressively lowered, so that a larger proportion of people's estates had to pay duties.

The records relating to death duty taxes and associated matters, are held in TNA, with indexes on the website. These records are particularly useful in giving the exact amount that an estate was worth. The death duty registers also contain further information, sometimes added for many years after the will was proved, such as the dates of death of individual beneficiaries, which will also help the family historian with research.

41

Inquests

If a person died in a way that gave rise to suspicions that the death might not have occurred naturally, then an inquest was held. In addition, inquests on all deaths in prison had to be held, even if it was obvious that the person had died from natural causes.

Even if your ancestor was very law-abiding he might have found himself, (or, more rarely, she might have found herself) imprisoned for debt. If he became ill and died while still in prison, an inquest would have been held and the results recorded in the prison inquest records, which makes such records always worth consulting.

ROLE OF THE CORONER

The office of coroner is first mentioned in 1174, though the post itself seems to be much older than that. The coroner had many legal and political responsibilities, but his main function was to look after the Crown's interests, especially in the event of a death. If a person was murdered, the murderer's property was forfeited to the Crown, so the death had to be investigated to see if any property or money could be confiscated. In medieval times the coroner had many duties, but over the centuries his responsibilities were gradually reduced.

OTHER INQUEST ROLES

There are a number of ways in which an ancestor might have been involved in an inquest, and so appear in the records, apart from being either the coroner or the deceased person.

Member of the jury

Once notified of a death that needed investigation, the coroner drew up a list of potential jurors. The parish beadle then visited the people on the list to call them to serve. Most of the jurymen were respectable tradesmen. Any compensation they received came out of public money, and they were not

ABOVE A coroner's inquest held at Charing Cross Hospital, London, in 1861. Inquests might also be held at inns, workhouses or prisons.

usually paid for their attendance before the first quarter of the 19th century. Even after this, individual counties had different practices (London did not pay until the end of the century). It was not, therefore, a popular duty, because they would lose business. Sometimes they paid substitutes to attend in their stead or simply pretended not to be at home when the beadle called.

Publican

Until the middle of the 19th century, the majority of inquests were held at a local inn, so, if you have publicans among your ancestors, it is possible that an inquest was held on their premises. Inquests were also held in hospitals and workhouses, which might have involved members of your family in some way.

Doctor

A doctor had to confirm the death and give an opinion about its cause.

Witness

People who had witnessed the death were called to give evidence. These could include members of the dead person's family, neighbours, friends, medical staff at hospitals, workhouse officials, prison workers and even passers-by.

EVIDENCE OF TREASURE-TROVE

The only other major example of the coroner's role in looking after the Crown's financial interests that survives to the present day is the investigation of treasure-trove. If a hoard of gold, silver or bullion is discovered and the owner cannot be identified, then a coroner must hold an inquest to determine whether it was accidentally lost, in which case it becomes the property of the finder, or if it was deliberately

hidden, in which case it becomes the property of the Crown. An ancestor's sudden increase in wealth might be due to hard work, an inheritance or gift, criminal activity or the discovery of treasure-trove. The latter is rare but still worth considering. There are papers relating to treasure-trove for 1825–1925 in TNA. Others should be with surviving inquest papers in CROs.

RESEARCHING INQUEST RECORDS

Whenever you go to a record office, check whether it has any surviving inquest papers. If a death took place in the parish where your ancestors were living at a particular time, it is worth checking to see whether a member of your family was involved as a juryman or, if any of them was an innkeeper, as the proprietor of the place where the inquest was held. They might also have given evidence.

When a verdict that resulted in a trial was passed, always follow this up in criminal records. Although the same evidence as was given at the inquest will be repeated, more evidence might have been discovered by the time the trial took place, so the criminal records will give you more information about what happened. You may also find that the trial jury passed a different verdict from that given at the inquest. There were a number of possible verdicts:

- "Visitation of God" (short for "Visitation of God by natural causes") was used for sudden deaths, such as from a heart attack or stroke.
- "Natural causes/natural death" was used to refer to long-standing illnesses such as tuberculosis, or diseases such as smallpox or cholera.
- "Mishap", "casual" or "misfortune" included in a verdict meant that the death was accidental.

- "Murder" and "manslaughter" are self-explanatory.
- "Justifiable homicide" was used when a person, such as a soldier, had grounds to believe that his life was in danger and so killed in self-defence.
- "Want of the necessities of life", which means starvation, shows how hard life could be for the poor.
- "Inclemency of the weather" (what we would call "exposure") might have been the verdict passed on a beggar who died outside on some frosty night or on someone who fell from his horse on his way home and died from the effects of cold.
- "Suicide". If the jury decided that the person had committed suicide, they had to decide whether he or she was sane at the time. People who were "lunatic" (as it was generally called) could be buried with full rites in a churchyard or burial ground. If, however, they were found to be in full possession of their faculties, a verdict of *felo de se* (literally, self-murderer) was passed. Until 1823, a *felo de se* suicide was buried at a crossroads, often with a stake through the body. After 1823, although the person could be buried in a churchyard, the burial had to take place between 9pm and midnight and was without a burial service. Until 1871 the suicide's property was forfeit to the Crown.

Where jurors could not decide why the death occurred, they passed an open verdict, such as "Found dead", or a narrative verdict, such as "Died from a fall".

FURTHER HELP

Gibson, Jeremy and Rogers, Colin
Coroners' Records (FHP)

Other Countries in the British Isles

The countries that make up the British Isles differ in ways that the researcher needs to know about, because they may affect the type of records that have been kept and where they are found today.

Welsh records

Wales has effectively been under British rule since medieval times, so the kinds of records found are the same as in England. The exception is land inheritance. By a Welsh tradition called "gavelkind", which ceased with the Act of Union of 1536, a man's property was divided between all his sons, rather than left to the eldest son. This led to people owning smaller and smaller parcels of land, which eventually became uneconomic and had to be sold. Since 1536, inheritance laws in England and Wales have been the same, so the family historian will find the same kinds of records in both countries.

INVESTIGATING BMD AND OTHER RECORDS

BMD certificates began in 1837, and the indexes are in the Family Record Centre (FRC). Other records are much the same as in England.

ABOVE Although Wales has a strong individual identity, in its public record keeping at least it is the same as England.

BELOW Carreg Cennen is one of the many castles built by Edward I of England in his efforts to rule Wales.

Parish records

Following the 1536 Act of Union, the law was the same in both countries, and therefore Welsh parish officials had the same duties and kept the same kinds of records in Wales as their counterparts did in England.

By the mid-19th century, some 80 per cent of the Welsh population was thought to belong to Nonconformist churches, mainly Methodist or Baptist, with a small Catholic community. This means that most of them will not be found in parish registers, apart from those that married between 1753 and 1837. They will, however, appear in other parish records, such as settlement and bastardy examinations, workhouse minutes, etc.

Wills

There are four bishops' dioceses in Wales: Bangor (including Anglesey), St Asaph, Llandaff and St David. Wills not proved in the Prerogative Court of Canterbury (PCC) were mainly proved in the diocesan courts. (The archdeaconry courts were less important for probate matters than in England.) Only in the archdeaconry of Brecon, in the see of St David, was there a consistory court proving wills. There was only one "peculiar" in Wales – the parish of Hawarden, Flintshire – which had the right to prove its own wills. Some Welsh parishes fell within the diocese of Hereford, so the wills of their inhabitants are kept in the Here-

Understanding Welsh family names

The small number of names shared by a majority of the population meant that many people acquired an extra name to distinguish them from other people with the same name in the same locality. This might be a mother's name, making hyphenated or double names quite common in Wales, or it might be a geographical location or an occupation, such as Jones of Mostyn or Jones the Baker. This helps the researcher to distinguish between individuals in records, but can become confusing with the next generation, since a child would not necessarily inherit the extra name but might acquire one of his or her own instead. This practice of using patronymics rather than fixed surnames did not fully die out until the advent of civil registration in 1837.

ford and Worcester County Record Office (CRO).

Only a small number of Welsh families remained Roman Catholic after the Reformation, but their numbers were swelled in the 19th century when many Irish Catholics came to the industrialized parts of Wales.

INTERPRETING THE LAW

Although Wales had its own legal system before the Act of Union in 1536, since that date the law has been the same as it is in England.

The Poor Laws

It seems that in Tudor times the Poor Laws operated only in Monmouthshire, and in many of the more sparsely populated parishes poor rates were not collected until 1755. The poverty stricken in many places therefore relied on charity and the support of landowners rather than parish relief. The Napoleonic Wars from the end of the 18th century led to an increase in the collection of rates.

Assize courts

From 1542 to its abolition in 1830, the Court of Great Session sat twice a year in each of the Welsh counties, with the exception of Monmouthshire, which was excluded from 1689. From 1831 there were two circuits, North and South Wales, and from 1945 Wales and Chester.

LOCATING RECORDS RELATING TO WELSH ANCESTORS

Since England and Wales have the same government, many of the official records relating to Wales are found in The National Archives (TNA).

Those searching for Welsh ancestry will find the National Library of Wales (NLW) is also a good starting point. Although the Welsh counties do have individual CROs, the NLW has copies of parish registers as well as diocesan records, court papers, newspapers and other material covering all the counties collected together in one place. Documents relating to manors, estates and other property in Wales may be here or in TNA.

RESEARCHING WELSH ANCESTORS

The ancient Palatinate of Cheshire, whose records are in TNA, included the old Welsh county of Flintshire, so it is possible you may find some relatives recorded there.

The area around the border between Wales and England is known as the Welsh Marches, and if your ancestors lived here, it is probably worth checking for missing ancestors in the records of the neighbouring English counties.

The Welsh courts went on returning coroners' inquests to the assize circuits well into the first part of the 19th century, long after the English courts ceased to do so. These records, which are in TNA, are therefore worth consulting for the genealogical information they might contain.

ABOVE Just as in England, Welsh counties have their own CROs, in which are held the wills of their inhabitants.

FURTHER HELP

Hamilton-Edwards, Gerald *In Search of Welsh Ancestry* (Phillimore)
National Library of Wales, Aberystwyth, Ceredigion SY23 3BU www.llgc.org.uk/. A reader's ticket is necessary to use the library. It is one of the copyright libraries in the British Isles, so publishers should have deposited a copy of all new books there.
Rowlands, John and Rowlands, Sheila *Welsh Family History: A Guide to Research* (FFHS)
Rowlands, John and Rowlands, Sheila *Second Stages in Researching Welsh Ancestry* (FFHS)

Scottish records

Before the Act of Union in 1707, Scotland had a separate parliament from England and Wales. After nearly 300 years, its own parliament was restored in 1999. Scotland had, and still has, a different legal system to the rest of Britain, which affects the types of records that are kept.

INVESTIGATING BMD AND OTHER RECORDS

Civil registration was introduced in 1855. Scottish certificates contain the same information as those south of the border, but with a few major, and useful, additions regarding BMD.

Birth certificates

On a child's birth certificate, the date and place of the parents' marriage is entered. This was dropped between 1856 and 1860. In the first year of registration (1855) only, the ages and birthplaces of both parents and details of their other children (if any) are recorded. All birth certificates also include the time of the child's birth, not just (as in England and Wales) if it was a multiple birth. For those genealogists who are interested in astrology, this presents an opportunity to have a full birth chart drawn up. There is an index of adopted children from 1930, though this does not contain the names of natural parents, and one of stillbirths from 1939, though the latter is not on open access.

Marriage certificates

The names of both parties' fathers and mothers (with maiden names) are included on marriage certificates. They also, until 1922, state whether

ABOVE Edinburgh's New Register House, designed by Robert Adam, holds BMD records and parish registers for Scotland.

the bride and groom were related and what the relationship was. In Scotland, a legal marriage could be contracted by agreement before witnesses or a sheriff, and the certificate will show whether the couple were married in church (the officiating minister would have signed the certificate) or by agreement. Certificates drawn up in 1855 only will also give details of previous marriages, any children and the birthplaces of both parties. There is a register of divorces from 1984.

Death certificates

In addition to the information given on death certificates in England and Wales, these contain the names of the deceased's father and mother (including her maiden name). In 1855, certificates also noted the deceased's birthplace and how long he or she had been resident in the place where they died, plus the names of spouses (including maiden names) and children, with their ages. For 1855–1861, details of the burial place and undertaker were noted.

Parish registers

When civil registration began in Scotland, the parish registers of the Church of Scotland parishes were called in. These are known as the Old Parochial Registers. Although some began in 1558, registers were generally not kept until about 1750 in the Highlands. Most were indexed by the original compilers, but in a variety of sometimes confusing and unhelpful ways. The Church of Jesus Christ of Latter-

Understanding Scottish family names

Before the 20th century, the Scots had a fairly standard pattern of naming children, which may give clues to the names of grandparents:
- eldest son was named after the paternal grandfather
- 2nd son was named after the maternal grandfather
- 3rd son was named after the father
- eldest daughter was named after the maternal grandmother

- 2nd daughter was named after the paternal grandmother
- 3rd daughter was named after the mother

It was also quite common to create girls' names by adding "-a" or "-ina" to a man's name, e.g. Jacoba, Jamesina, which in some cases seems to have been done when there weren't enough sons in the family to commemorate the male relatives.

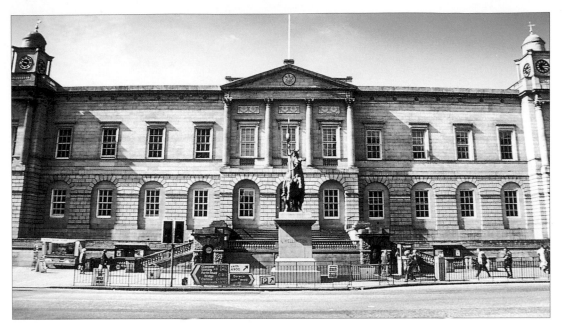

ABOVE The National Records of Scotland in Edinburgh, formerly the Scottish Records Office, holds a wealth of material on Scottish ancestors.

day Saints (LDS) has produced an index of baptisms and marriages, and the original parish registers can be seen on the government's Scotland's People website. Some do not include the actual details of a service but do, in the case of marriage, include notice of the intention to marry.

The registers contain relatively few burial records, but might have a note about the hiring of the mort cloth – a cloth to cover a body. They do, however, usually give the names of godparents in the entry for a baptism.

Many Scots were Nonconformists, mainly Presbyterian. There was also a strong Catholic presence in Scotland, particularly among those of Irish origin who migrated in the 19th century.

Testamentary records

The inheritance of land and buildings in Scotland was according to laid-down rules, not the owner's personal whim. This meant that only movable property could be left at death, with the details recorded in a document called the testament.

Before 1823, Scotland was divided into areas called commissariots, which were roughly the equivalent of a bishop's diocese, where testaments were proved. The Commissariot of Edinburgh had both local and national jurisdiction, as well as over those Scots who died overseas. Most testaments have been indexed. If heirs were under the age of majority, the commissary courts could appoint guardians of their interests, called tutors. Even though rules on inheritance were clear-cut, there could be disputes about the provisions of a testament, which would be heard in the court in which the wills were proved.

If someone died intestate, a testament dative, including an inventory of the deceased's possessions, was drawn up. A notice, called an edict, might be nailed to the church door requesting anyone who had an interest in the deceased's goods to attend a commissary court hearing. These notices appear in commissary court records, to which other documents relative to the matter should be attached.

Sheriff Courts took over the administration of testaments in 1823 and continued to do so until 1876, when a national system was instituted.

Armorial bearings

The Lord Lyon King of Arms has jurisdiction over all matters relating to armorial bearings, and the records of the Lyon Court contain much information about pedigrees. Ancient heraldic material is often worth researching, as it is not only the wealthy and nobility who are entitled to bear and apply for arms.

ABOVE The interior of the impressive dome of the National Records of Scotland.

The Poor Laws

Before 1845, the Scottish Poor Laws were administered by parish officials, and references to relief may be found in the minutes of Kirk Sessions. After 1845, Parochial Boards were set up in each parish. Lists of people receiving assistance in their homes and those who had entered the poorhouse were compiled. Some children, invalids and lunatics were placed in private homes to be cared for, and the board made reports on them.

Courts

The lowest level of criminal courts is the Sheriff Court (which also had jurisdiction over some civil matters). Appeals from here went to the High Court of Justiciary (the highest criminal court in Scotland), which dealt with serious crimes. The statements of witnesses, called precognitions, are held in the records of the Lord Advocate's Department, but there might be copies of some with the papers of the Sheriff Court. There are few surviving precognitions before 1812.

In some places, a particular person held a franchise from the Crown that gave him jurisdiction over both civil and criminal matters in a specified area.

Before the Act of Union in 1707, which led to its abolition in the following year, the Scottish Privy Council dealt with criminal cases, generally among the higher echelons of society. The Admiralty Court, abolished in 1830, had jurisdiction over the high seas and harbours.

Fatal accident inquiries

Scotland does not have coroners. Any deaths that resulted in legal action will be found in the criminal courts following an investigation by the Sheriff, but there will not be official documents related to suicide or misadventure.

Service of Heirs and Register of Sasines

The Service of Heirs relates to the inheritance of property other than land and generally states the relationship of the person who inherited it to the deceased. The Register of Sasines relates to the inheritance of land and dates from 1617.

These are the major differences to be found between family records in England and Wales and those in Scotland. Other information relating to family history, such as apprenticeships, freemen, criminal and civil proceedings, will be found in the equivalent Scottish records.

INTERPRETING THE LAW

Scotland has a separate legal system from the rest of the UK. The differences of most interest to genealogists relate to wills and inheritance of property, but other areas, like family law, will need to be considered and investigated when doing research.

From 1848 there are records in the Lord Advocate's department of inquiries into accidents, and after 1895 Sheriff Courts had, by law, to conduct inquiries into fatal accidents.

LOCATING RECORDS RELATING TO SCOTTISH ANCESTORS

The genealogist tracing Scottish ancestry has a great advantage over those researching in England, because there is often more detail given about relationships. Also, all the most frequently used family history data (parish registers, testamentary records, etc.) have been digitized and put on to the government's Scotlands People site. On the Scotlands Places website are copies of 17th–19th century tax rolls, Ordnance Survey name books, maps and plans.

On 1 April 2011, the General Register Office for Scotland merged with the National Archives of Scotland (NAS) to become the National Records of Scotland (NRS). The records are split on two adjoining sites. The Scotlands People Centre, a public search facility in General Register House, has computer access to all the digitized records. Next door are the historical and legal search rooms where national and local government records, court and legal documents, business archives and adoption records can be consulted. There is a computer link from the public search room to those records in the historical and legal search rooms, which have been digitized. These include the registers of some Nonconformist congregations and also the Minutes of Kirk Sessions, which contain information

FURTHER HELP

ScotlandPeople
www.scotlandspeople.gov.uk
ScotlandPlaces
www.scotlandsplaces.gov.uk
Scottish Association of Family History Societies
www.safhs.org.uk
National Records of Scotland (NRS), H M General Register House, 2 Princes Street, Edinburgh, EH1 3YY
www.nrscotland.gov.uk
Clarke, Tristram *Tracing Your Scottish Ancestors: the Official Guide* (Birlinn/ National Records of Scotland)
Durie, Bruce *Scottish Genealogy* (The History Press)
Relatively Clear: a search guide for adopted people in Scotland (Birthlink)
Raymond, Stuart A. *Scottish Family History on the Web: a directory* (Family History Partnership)

about illegitimacy, irregular marriages, claims for poor relief and the like.

The minor records online include a Marine Register of births from 1855, listing the births of children on British-registered vessels if the father was Scottish. There are also registers of BMD in foreign countries during 1860–1965; in the High Commissioner's Returns of BMD from 1964; in Air Registers of Births and Deaths from 1948; in Service Records from 1881; in Consular Returns of BMD from 1914 and in Foreign Marriages from 1947.

Records in Scotland are generally closed for 75 years. It is worth noting that in the past it was common for women to keep their maiden names after marriage, so it's worth checking for both names if researching a woman. After 1707, the armed forces covered the whole of the British Isles, so records relating to Scottish soldiers, sailors and airmen will be found in The National Archives of England.

ABOVE Despite being housed in a historic building, the National Records of Scotland has modern facilities and a vast collection of records.

Irish records

The family historian researching Irish ancestry faces a number of problems. The first is that the majority of the population was Roman Catholic, and their registers did not begin until late in the 18th century. The second is the relatively few number of surnames shared by most of the population. The third is that the Irish Public Record Office, housed in Four Courts, Dublin, was destroyed by protestors against British rule in 1922. Very few of the contents, which included about half the Church of Ireland parish registers, census returns, wills and other government records, survived.

ABOVE Four Courts, Dublin, had many of its records destroyed during the 1922 uprising.

INVESTIGATING BMD AND OTHER RECORDS

After 1922, BMD records are complete but, as the country was then divided into two, these and other records are in different places.

Civil registration

Civil registration of all BMD began in Ireland in 1864, but non-Catholic marriages were registered only from 1845 onwards. The partition of Ireland has meant duplication of material between the two General Register Offices. Records up to 1922 are held in the General Register Office in Roscommon. After that date, it holds copies of records in Northern Ireland. The GRO (Northern Ireland), in Belfast, is a separate register office. It holds BMD records for Northern Ireland from 1922 onwards and copies of indexes to pre-1922 events. There are also Marine, Consular, and Foreign Marriage Registers of BMD relating to Irish people at sea or overseas in

both offices. After 1922, laws on registration of events such as stillbirth, adoption and illegitimate children were different in Eire and Northern Ireland.

Parish registers

The Church of Ireland served a small percentage of the population, mainly the Protestant middle and upper classes. As mentioned above, about half their registers from before 1870 had been deposited in the Dublin Public Record Office and were destroyed. However, others had remained in their own churches; some transcripts of these had been made before the registers were surrendered, and others had already been published. The surviving material, in addition to parish accounts and other documents, are scattered among various locations. The records of parishes that no longer exist, for example, have been deposited in the library of the Representative Church Body.

Between 1915 and 1922, proof of age in order to claim benefits might be extracted from Church of Ireland parish registers, and the forms to do this, which contain parents' names, are preserved in the National Archives.

Unlike the Church of Ireland, the Roman Catholic Church did not have a role in local government, and so it did not need to keep registers in the same way. Most baptisms and marriages took place in the priest's home or in the home of the family. Catholic registers did not begin until the middle of the 18th century in towns and the 19th century in rural areas. Most original registers remain with their churches, but the majority has been copied on to films, which are held in the National Library. Some burials of Catholics took place in Church of Ireland burial grounds, depending on the attitude of the minister.

Other denominations, such as the Nonconformists (Baptists, Congregationalists, Huguenots, Lutherans,

Methodists, Moravians, Presbyterians and Quakers) and Jews, kept their own records. Although all the original registers of the Huguenot churches were destroyed in 1922, they had already been published. Other records are deposited in various archives or remain with their congregations, but many have also been copied.

Wills

Between 1536 and 1858, wills were proved in Church of Ireland ecclesiastical courts. The senior court was the Prerogative Court of Armagh, which had jurisdiction over all the commissary courts (there were no archdeaconry courts in Ireland) but was inferior to the PCC. People with property in both Ireland and England would therefore have had their wills proved in the PCC, and those records are in the Family Record Centre in London.

After 1858, the proving of wills was taken over by the government. Transcript copies of wills proved in local registries were passed to Dublin, where an annual index was made. The original wills, before and after 1858, were deposited at Four Courts, and so destroyed in 1922, but the indexes, which give some useful information, have survived and so have the post-1858 transcript copies from the registries outside Dublin.

Between 1858 and 1876, the Principal Probate Registry in London had an additional section at the end of its indexes, which included some Irish probate records dealing with people who owned property in both Ireland and England.

INTERPRETING THE LAW

Ireland had its own parliament, but all of its activities had to be approved by the British government. Although the majority of the population was Roman Catholic, laws were passed at various times to penalize them and prevent them from holding office of any kind. This discrimination finally ended in 1829, although some provisions had been repealed at different times before that date.

Land records

The paucity of registers and the destruction of many documents mean that much information about Irish family history will come from records relating to land tenure. Most land in Ireland was owned by a relatively small number of people and let out on leases. Private estate papers may contain information about tenants. Because they are private papers, they may be with the original owners or in a number of repositories in Ireland or mainland Britain. During the famine years, many landowners abandoned their properties and left Ireland.

Registry of Deeds

The Registry of Deeds was set up in 1708, primarily to stop Catholics acquiring land. A variety of documents, including wills, land transfer documents, mortgages, marriage settlement letters and share sales, are included in these records. They mainly relate to upper-class Anglo-Irish families, and so are not typical of the average inhabitant. Registration was not compulsory, so not every transaction will be here.

As the laws on Catholics were relaxed towards the end of the 18th century, more people were able to lease or own land. The records are in the Registry of Deeds, in Dublin, where there is an index containing abstracts of the documents.

Ejectment books

Before a landlord could eject tenants from his property, he had to obtain a court judgement, and ejectment books summarizing these cases provide much information of use to genealogists, especially those whose ancestors emigrated. Not all have survived (there seem to be none, for example, from Northern Ireland), but they are worth checking out.

The famine of the 1840s created a huge increase in ejectments, but this was not entirely a case of hard-hearted

ABOVE The Irish potato famine led to widespread poverty and eviction.

51

landlords throwing out starving people. The landlords had to pay rates on their land, and, in order to help the increasing number of poor, the amounts rose. Those with land-owning ancestors may find their problems reflected in ejectment books.

The Incumbered Estate Court

From 1849, if bankruptcy resulted, the landlords' estates were disposed of in the Incumbered Estate Court, which dealt with the auction of lands. This was renamed the Landed Estates Court in 1858. In 1877, it became part of the Chancery Division of the High Court in Ireland. Here it was called the Land Judges' Court, and continued until 1880. Records are in the National Archives of Ireland. Much valuable information, including maps, is given in the sales catalogues (called rentals) produced when landowners had to sell, these are in the National Archives, the National Library or the Public Record Office of Northern Ireland (PRONI).

Other sources

Ireland possesses records giving the same kinds of genealogical information as the rest of the British Isles, such as courts, apprenticeships, freemen, commercial and trade directories, and so on. Newspapers and magazines, especially the *Hibernian*, will provide additional facts, but it is mainly the well-to-do and criminal classes that are recorded in them.

Tithe Plotment Books

Compiled in the 1820s and 1830s, Tithe Plotment Books cover landowners and primary tenants in parishes. The LDS has filmed these records, so they are available through their Family History Centres and in a number of record offices.

BELOW After eviction, an Irish peasant would have little with which to start again.

Griffith's Primary Valuation

Information about landowners and occupiers in the mid-19th century was issued in stages for 1848–1864. This publication's official title is *General Valuation of Rateable Property*, but it is generally known as Griffith's Primary Valuation, after the commissioner who was responsible for carrying it out. The surveys largely took place after the Irish famine, and so are valuable for allowing the family historian to see who survived or remained in Ireland. Almost every head of a household is listed in these surveys.

Land Commission

The 1881 Land Act set up the Land Commission, which originally determined fair rents. Its work developed into helping tenants purchase their property. These records are currently in the Irish National Archives, but public access to them is restricted. A summary of the Commission's documents is held in the National Library.

LOCATING RECORDS RELATING TO IRISH ANCESTORS

Listing where in Ireland your ancestors were before and after 1922 will make locating records easier.

Census returns

A few records of censuses before 1901 survived the 1922 destruction: there are fragments from 1821, 1831, 1841 and 1851. The pre-1851 censuses in Ireland contained more information than their English or Scottish equivalents. In addition to the original records, there are some forms relating to information from searches made in the census records, which were used by elderly people to prove their ages in order to claim old age pensions after 1908. The 1901 and 1911 censuses survived and are on the PRONI website, but you need to know where your ancestors were living in those years.

Heritage Centres

The increasing growth of interest in family history led to the setting up of Genealogical Indexing Centres, also called Heritage Centres, around Ireland. These centres index and computerize church registers and other records in their area. The public is not allowed access to the databases, but information from them is provided for a fee. They are useful if you know at least the county from which your ancestors came.

Service records

Records for the Irish branches of the armed services are in TNA.

Education records

Charter schools began in 1731, and by the beginning of the 19th century there were a variety of private, Church and "hedge" schools in Ireland. Hedge schools, which dated from medieval times, educated children in Gaelic, which was the first language of most Irish people until the 19th century. They declined for a number of reasons: the growth of state-run education, which was in English; the recognition that, in order to succeed professionally, people needed to speak English; and the emigration of many of the poorer Irish citizens.

The National Board of Education (Ireland) began state-run schools in 1831. Information from school logbooks, where they survive, can substitute for the destroyed censuses. Although the schools were non-denominational, their records include a note of the children's religions. When and why children left the school is also entered, and this may give useful information about families who emigrated.

ABOVE IRA forces fought a bitter struggle with the British in the streets of Dublin in 1922.

Records of graduates from Ireland's main universities have been published. Roman Catholics were barred from universities until 1793, but some did receive a university education and are noted as "RC" in the registers.

FURTHER HELP

General Register Office, Government Offices, Convent Road, Roscommon, Eire www.groireland.ie

General Register Office (NI), Oxford House, 49–55 Chichester Street, Belfast BT1 4HL www.nidirect.gov.uk/gro

National Archives of Ireland, Bishop Street, Dublin 8, Eire www.nationalarchives.ie

Public Record Office of Northern Ireland, 2 Titanic Boulevard, Belfast BT3 9HQ www.proni.gov.uk

TNA's *Royal Irish Constabulary* holds records from 1816-1922

Grenham, John *Tracing Your Irish Ancestors* (Gill & Macmillan)

Raymond, Stuart A. *Irish Family History on the Web*

Flyleaf Press www.flyleaf.ie for publications on Irish counties

RESEARCHING IRISH ANCESTORS

The destruction in 1922 of Four Courts in Dublin, which contained centralized records, means that it is essential to find out where in Ireland your ancestors originated. If they emigrated to England, Wales Scotland, or overseas, this may come from census returns (although many people simply entered "Ireland" on the return) and settlement examinations. Those who entered the armed services will also have their birthplace entered in records. It is worth remembering that the Republic of Ireland was neutral during World War II.

When civil registration was introduced in 1864, a fine was payable if a birth was not registered within three months, so poor people might have adjusted the date of a child's birth to avoid a penalty. Roman Catholics would, however, have had the child baptized within a few days of birth, either at the priest's house or their own home, so it is worth cross-referencing the civil and church records if you can.

Channel Islands records

There are no copies of the parish records online but IGI coverage of the Channel Islands births and marriage is virtually complete. The Channel Islands came under British rule with the accession of William the Conqueror in 1066, and they retained both a system of law very different from that of England, especially in respect of land inheritance, and a form of French as the inhabitants' first language. As a result, the majority of earlier records are in French.

Many of the inhabitants were involved in the fishing industry. Their proximity to the West Country of England, where fishing was also a major industry, means that there was a fair amount of interchange.

A number of Huguenots emigrated from France to the Channel Islands, and refugees from the French Revolution also settled there. Although the islands have their own dialect, the language was similar enough for them to have integrated easily.

LEFT The castle above Gorey Harbour in Jersey was built to defend the island from seaborne invasion.

BELOW LEFT The French failed to gain control of the Channel Islands in the late 18th century.

During the French and Napoleonic Wars, the islands were heavily garrisoned to keep them out of French hands. A number of soldiers and sailors married local women. A local militia was also raised, and many of its records are in TNA. During World War II, the Channel Islands were occupied by the Germans. There are a number of books on this period.

Guernsey

Civil registration of births, deaths and non-Anglican marriages began in 1840, but all marriages did not have to be registered until 1919.

During the 19th century, accounts of strangers, or etrangers, were kept, which included passenger lists. These will be found among the constable's records in each parish.

The island's Archives Office, the Greffe, contains the registers of BMD and wills from 1841. It also contains the records of St Peter Port's Hospital, which was built in 1741 and served both as a place to treat the sick and a workhouse. The records cover 1741-1900. Records for the prison, known as the House of Separation, also survive.

Jersey

Civil registration of BMD began in 1842. Before that date, information was recorded in parish registers. Jersey has separate archives for civil registration from 1842 (which are in the Superintendent Registrar's) and other records (in the Judicial Greffe).

Before 1602, matters concerning land were arranged verbally in front of witnesses, generally after church services. The Land Registry was then set up to document transactions. On the death of a landowner, his estate would

be divided between his children, with the eldest son receiving the largest share. Wills of Realty, relating to land and buildings, date from 1851 and are deposited at the Land Registry, while Wills of Personality, covering money and movable goods, are in the Probate Registry. Both have been filmed by the LDS. Legal courts covered inheritance, crime, civil cases, small debts and bankruptcy.

Refugees from the French Revolution in 1789 came to Jersey. They established a Roman Catholic congregation, which was later joined by an influx of Irish immigrants. Many of these left for America from the 1870s, when there were financial problems and the work dried up in the Channel Islands. A chapel was built in 1825 and two other churches in 1867 and 1877. The surviving registers of all three have been transcribed and deposited in the Channel Islands Family History Society's archives and the Société Jersiaise. There is an index.

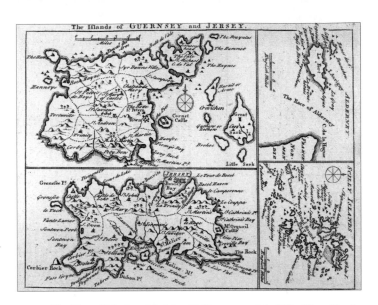

ABOVE The Channel Islands and the Isles of Scilly are some of the UK's offshore islands.

FURTHER HELP

Channel Islands Family History Society (CIFHS), PO Box 507, Jersey JE4 5TN
www.jerseyfamilyhistory.org
Archives are located in the Jersey Museum, The Weighbridge, St Helier, Jersey, JE2 3NG
www.jerseyheritage.org
Guernsey's historical and family history research centre is at Priaulx Library, Candie Road, St Peter Port, Guernsey GY1 1ED
www.priaulxlibrary.co.uk
The Société Guernesiaise covers aspects of history, natural history and conservation on Guernsey, Alderney and Sark. It has a family history section. PO Box 314, St Peter Port, Guernsey, GY1 3TG www.societe.org.gg
Backhurst, Marie-Louise *Tracing Your Channel Islands Ancestors* (Pen & Sword)

Alderney

The civil registration of births and deaths dates from 1850, and marriages from 1886.

Many of Alderney's earlier records seem to have been destroyed during the German occupation in World War I. Those that have survived (apart from censuses) have been copied by a local volunteer. Enquiries are routed through the Greffe in Guernsey.

Sark

The island of Sark was uninhabited until 1563, when the Seigneur of St Ouen in Jersey moved there with his family, and a number of followers, to prevent it from being taken over by the French during the Wars of Religion. They were joined by other people from Guernsey and Jersey and a few from the English mainland. A small Huguenot community established itself there in 1570.

To this day, the island still has a feudal system of land tenure. Inheritance laws are very strict, so relatively few people have ever made wills. The records of Sark are accessed through the Greffe in Guernsey. Civil registration of deaths began in 1915, marriages in 1919 and births in 1925.

RECORDS RELATING TO ANCESTORS FROM THE CHANNEL ISLANDS

Although there are copies locally, TNA holds census returns. It also has some records of BMD notified to the British authorities between 1831 and 1958. The Chelsea and Greenwich Hospitals' records contain information about retired soldiers and sailors living in the Channel Islands and receiving a pension from them.

A particularly useful source for information is the Association Oath Rolls of 1696 for Guernsey and Jersey, since they constitute a virtual census of the adult male population of the islands at that date. There are also documents relating to the rental of Crown lands in Alderney for 1832–1961.

Isle of Man records

The Isle of Man was ruled by Norsemen from the 10th century, until the King of Norway sold it to Scotland in 1266. In 1341, it came under English control, but the feudal system of land and property laws remained in force until 1867. Tenants paid for land owned by their lords by handing over part of the produce of their holding and by doing work for the landowner.

The Isle of Man is self-governing and levies its own taxes. Its legislative body, the Tynwald, is divided into an upper and a lower house. Otherwise, the Isle of Man came under English rule, so the administrative system of parishes is the same. It forms the diocese of the Bishop of Sodor and Man.

Manx, a form of Gaelic, was spoken on the island until the 18th century, but legal and official documents were written in English. This language gradually took over, hastened by the

ABOVE The Isle of Man's ancient Scandanavian heritage is celebrated at the annual Viking Festival.

BELOW Viking ship-burials are no longer practised, only recreated at festivals commemorating the Isle of Man's past.

introduction in 1872 of free elementary schools, where the teaching was in English. The last mother-tongue speakers died in the 1940s.

INVESTIGATING BMD

Civil registration of births and deaths began in 1878 and of marriages in 1884. From 1849 there are some certificates of Nonconformists' marriages, obtained by those who did not wish to be married in a parish church. Wills were proved in ecclesiastical courts until 1884, when a system of civil probate was instituted. There are no birth, marriage or death records for the Isle of Man available to see online but the parish register coverage on the IGI is virtually complete.

Property records

As elsewhere in the United Kingdom, property records are a vital source of information about Manx ancestry. The Isle of Man's feudal system of land tenure means that land records are essentially the same as manorial records. They are recorded in books called Libri (from the Latin for books): Libri Assedationis contain rent rolls, while Libri Vastarum contain details of admissions of landowners to property and the fines and rents they paid.

Composition Books contain descriptions of individual holdings and fines paid on them. They were no longer kept after 1704, when some of the more feudal rights of the lord were removed, though some remained.

Newspapers

Local newspapers started around the beginning of the 19th century. Before then, the *Cumberland Pacquet* carried some Manx news. Copies are held in the Heritage Library, as well as in the British Library Newspaper Library at Colindale in London.

LOCATING RECORDS RELATING TO ANCESTORS FROM THE ISLE OF MAN

The National Archives holds records of the Isle of Man's government and government employees, armed services, and assize records. It also has documents relating to land rented from the Crown for 1832–1954 and pensions paid to ex-servicemen living there. It may also hold wills of inhabitants proved in the PCC before 1858.

The Manx National Heritage Library is the equivalent of the CRO and holds copies of the surviving church registers, which are all indexed on the International Genealogical Index (IGI), as well as copies of the census returns (the originals are in TNA, and online). The 1881 census is

recorded on the CD-ROMs produced by the LDS. The Heritage Library also holds copies of wills before 1910 and property records, including a large collection of deeds between the late 17th century and 1910, which were enrolled with the local courts. Wills proved after 1916 are in the Registry, as are deeds after 1910.

When plans to destroy the majority of Merchant Navy crew lists held at the Registry of Shipping and Seamen were announced, due to lack of space, the Heritage Library managed to save those relating to Manx ports, and these have now been indexed. In addition to Manxmen, there are many sailors from Ireland and Scotland in these records.

During the World Wars, there were internment camps on the Isle of Man holding German and Italian men. The records, and fact sheets, are in TNA.

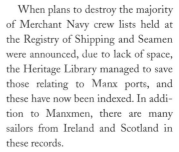

ABOVE Germans in a camp at Douglas during World War I. These internees were kept occupied by making brooms.

LEFT Mooragh camp, an internment camp set up during World War II, is now a public park.

FURTHER HELP

Douglas Civil Registry Deemsters Walk, Bucks Road, Douglas, Isle of Man, IM1 3AR www.gov.im/ registries/general/civilregistry/
There is an index for BMD registration 1877-1979, which is being compiled by volunteers on www.manxbmd.com
The National Library and Archives is situated at the Manx Museum, Douglas, Isle of Man IM1 3LY www.manxnationalheritage.im
Isle of Man FHS family history library can be found at Derby Lodge, Derby Road, Peel IM5 1HH www.iomfhs.im

Working Lives

Most of our ancestors worked long hours for many years – there were no old age pensions or an official retirement age until the 20th century.

Education

Before the 20th century, relatively few people needed to be able to read and write, since there were plenty of jobs that did not need literacy or numeracy. Indeed, many of the upper classes resisted plans to educate the poor, fearing that teaching them these skills would make them dissatisfied with their lives and lead to social unrest.

PRIMARY AND SECONDARY EDUCATION

Education was, until comparatively recently, not seen as the responsibility of the state. It was up to individuals to arrange for their children's education, and there were a variety of different ways to deliver it.

Early schools

There was a strongly defined hierarchy to the education provided for children in the past. Grammar schools, many of which were founded in the 16th century under Edward VI, and public schools, such as Eton, had originally been intended for poor children but were quickly taken over by the rich. The better-off sections of society employed tutors or governesses for their children. Among the middle and lower classes, it was mothers who were expected to teach their children to read and write. The children of tradesmen also learned account-keeping, either from their parents or from someone paid to teach them.

There were, in addition, a variety of schools, most of which were established as charitable foundations by either an individual or a religious organization, such as the Society for Promoting Christian Knowledge. Many had distinctive uniforms, such as the blue coats and yellow stockings of Christ's Hospital in London. Cathedrals also had (and still have) schools for choristers, who were, until the end of the 20th century, always male. Nonconformists also established schools to educate their children. What all schools had in common was that they based their education on religious faith.

There were a few occupational schools before the 19th century. Most of these, such as Christ's Hospital in London, were connected with the sea. Although most pupils at this establishment had a general education, the boys in the mathematical school were specifically prepared for their apprenticeship to sea captains.

Schools in the 19th century

Dame schools, usually run by a single woman, started from the 1830s. The standard of teaching was variable: some were little more than child-minding services so that mothers could work, but others did provide a basic education, mainly in reading and, for girls, sewing. It was not until the beginning of the 19th century that proposals for a national system of education were made. The first was in 1802, but the government was reluctant to get involved until 1870, when the Education Act obliged local authorities to provide education, which was made compulsory.

Schools to educate children and young people who had committed petty crimes or who were deemed likely to get into trouble were started around the beginning of the 19th cen-

LEFT Sunday schools, set up by churches, were another source of education for poor children.

58

tury. In addition, Magdelen Hospitals, which attempted to reform prostitutes, often educated the women they took in, many of whom were very young, then tried to place them as servants.

Other establishments, known as reformatories, Certified Industrial Schools or Day Industrial Schools, educated children and trained them in a skill that would help them to obtain employment. In 1933, they were renamed Approved Schools.

Schools in the 20th century

The 20th century brought various changes in education, but these largely built on the work done in the 19th century. The major difference was the 1944 Education Act, which made primary and secondary education free to all, and set up grammar, technical and secondary modern schools for children over 11. Comprehensive schools, from

A WORD IN SEASON.

ABOVE After 1887, delinquents could be sent to special schools instead of prison.

the 1970s, no longer divided children according to academic ability.

The place of girls

Most education was given to boys, because they were expected to earn a living, in order to support their families, when they grew up. Girls' education was considered to be of secondary importance. Small private schools, some of which took boarders, taught girls accomplishments designed to help them attract a husband. These were set up from the late 18th century and taught reading and writing; some history and geography; a little fashionable French and/or German; and a musical instrument, usually the piano. During the 19th century, the number of these schools increased, but it wasn't until the end of the century that a few with academic ambitions for girls were started. The number increased throughout the 20th century as the need for women to earn a living, both before and after marriage, was recognized.

Significant dates in the history of primary and secondary education

1780 Sunday School Movement began.

1802 Act for the Education of Apprentices stated that apprentices should have at least an hour a week's religious instruction on Sunday. They were to be examined by the parish minister.

1810 Ragged Schools, free to very poor children and orphans, began. They encouraged practical skills and expected their pupils to earn money from a very early age by cleaning shoes or running errands.

1811 National Society for the Promotion and Education of the Poor founded with the aim of providing a school in every parish.

1814 British and Foreign Schools Society founded to provide schools with a Nonconformist ethos.

1833 The government awarded a

grant of £20,000 to introduce denominational schools. In 1839, inspectors were appointed to ensure that the money was being properly spent. The grant was increased in 1850, 1858 and 1861, when pupil teachers were introduced. These were bright pupils who were paid to work and train as teachers for five years, getting a certificate for each year successfully completed.

1857 Industrial Schools set up to educate delinquents in a trade. They were also called reformatories.

1861 Payment by results introduced. Schools received 4s for each pupil who attended and 2s 8d for each subject passed by each child in the annual examinations. This led to a national syllabus.

1870 Education Act made education compulsory for children

under 10. It was free to the poor, but others paid a small weekly fee.

1893 School leaving age raised to 11.

1899 School leaving age raised to 12.

1902 Local Education Authorities (LEAs) replaced the old School Boards and received increased powers.

1908 Borstals for delinquent children replaced reformatories.

1944 Education Act created grammar, technical and secondary modern schools. The 11-plus examination was introduced to decide which type of school each child should attend.

1947 School leaving age raised to 15.

1974 School leaving age raised to 16.

Locating school records

From 1862, all schools had to keep logbooks, and references to individual pupils can be found in them. You may also find admission books and attendance registers, which were begun in order to record the number of pupils. Some local authorities gave awards for good attendance.

The managers of the school (later known as the governors) kept minute books, which may also have survived. These deal largely with administrative matters and should include information about children punished for bad behaviour. School magazines and ex-pupils associations' newsletters may provide further useful information.

Some school records remain with the schools themselves; others have been deposited in County Record Offices (CROs), and those for Church schools may be located through the denomination's archives. Dr Williams's Library holds information on some Nonconformist schools. Many of the registers of the early grammar, charity and more up-market schools, such as Wellington and Haileybury, have also been published.

Researching school records

The following points should help you in your research:

- In census returns, school children were noted as "scholars".
- If your ancestors lived in a large town or city, you may find directories useful to locate the nearest school to their home, then find the records.
- As well as the child's date of birth, father's name, address and previous school, admission books usually record the date and reason a child left, if this was before the school-leaving age. This could give clues to when your ancestors moved house.
- Events in schools are usually well reported in local newspapers from the end of the 19th century.
- Many schools have honours boards, which list pupils who went on to higher or further education, and Rolls of Honour, which list ex-pupils and teachers who died while serving in the World Wars.

TERTIARY EDUCATION

Before the 19th century, any form of higher education at universities was the preserve of the wealthy or the very clever, who managed to get scholarships, although this would only be with considerable support from a teacher or patron. Most universities and some colleges have published lists of their graduates.

Universities

Until 1836, there were only two universities in England: Oxford and Cambridge. Scotland had four: St Andrews, Glasgow, Edinburgh and Aberdeen, and there was one, Trinity College, Dublin, in Ireland. These all had their origins before 1600. Those people who could not accept the tenets of the established Church, such as Nonconformists, Roman Catholics, Jews and others, were barred from these universities. If your ancestors were not members of the Church of England, they are unlikely to have gone to the established universities, so you need to look elsewhere for records of their tertiary education.

Catholic tertiary education

Catholics often sent their children to the Continent for both secondary and tertiary education. Some lists of

ABOVE St Paul's School in London had an imposing classroom where boys received a classical education.

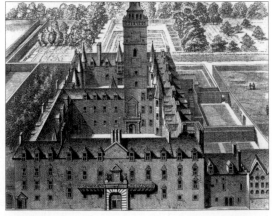

ABOVE The great respect for education in Scotland meant that Glasgow University was one of four founded here before 1600.

Significant dates in the history of tertiary education

The list of institutions included here is not exhaustive: many large hospitals trained doctors and nurses, for example. Also, all the many denominational colleges are excluded.

1167 Oxford University founded.

1209 Cambridge University founded.

1411 St Andrews in Scotland founded.

1451 University of Glasgow founded.

1495 University of Aberdeen founded.

1583 University of Edinburgh founded.

1593 Trinity College, Dublin founded.

1663 First Dissenting Academy founded.

1799 Royal Military College Sandhurst set up to train Army officers.

1804 East India Company started two establishments – one for its army, the other for its civil servants.

1820s Mechanics Institutes and Working Men's Institutes started to hold classes in the evenings for men. Most were on technical subjects to help them progress at work, but there were also lectures on cultural matters.

1844 Royal Agricultural College, Cirencester, founded.

1855 The Jews' College (later renamed the London School of Jewish Studies) founded to train Orthodox rabbis. It is now part of the University of London.

1869 Girton College for women founded. It moved to Cambridge University in 1873.

1879 Lady Margaret Hall and Somerville, the first two women's colleges of Oxford University, founded.

1889 Technical Instruction Act made provision for the establishment of part-time and evening classes to provide technical and occupational qualifications.

1903 Founding of the Workers Educational Association.

Catholics who graduated overseas have been published by the Catholic Record Society.

Nonconformist tertiary education

A few Dissenting Academies were established after the mid-17th century, and from the 18th century more and more Nonconformists founded their own denominational colleges and academies. Most were started to train clergymen, but others existed to provide a university-level education for those who, for religious reasons, could not go to the established universities. London University started out by awarding degrees gained through a number of colleges and institutions, such as the Inns of Court and medical schools, which later joined together under its aegis.

The admittance of women

Towards the end of the 19th century, women began the fight to enter higher education, and colleges for them were founded within universities.

Teacher training colleges

Pupil teachers in elementary (now primary) schools started work at about 14. Some were apprentices, but most were simply children in the school who showed an interest in and aptitude for teaching.

The first established teacher training college for primary school teachers was started in Glasgow in 1837. From the early 1900s, Local Education Authorities set up day training colleges, and universities established departments of education, which catered for both primary and secondary school teachers.

Alternative further education

Before the advent of grants for tertiary education, most working-class people could not attend university. Even if a child was able to get a scholarship, poor families depended on their children's income, and so needed them to work. The answer was night school. Most of these first night schools taught commercial practical skills that would improve the students' job opportunities, but the Workers Educational Associations aimed to provide classes in a variety of subjects for those who had not been able to pursue their education while younger.

FURTHER HELP

TNA has a fact sheet about researching school archives and it also holds a number of records of individual schools. Many will be in CROs or local studies libraries.

Most of the large public schools in England have published their own histories, and records of their pupils, many of which have been put on CD-Rom.

Private schools are most difficult to find – try Access to Archives on www.nationalarchives.gov.uk/a2a. Chapman, Colin R. *Basic Facts About ... Using Education Records* (FHP)

Apprenticeships

The majority of children started work between the ages of 12 and 14. Many went into domestic service (before World War I this was how most people began their working lives), but others were apprenticed to learn a trade.

APPRENTICESHIPS BEFORE THE 19TH CENTURY

In 1563, the Statute of Artificers laid down that no one could practise a certain occupation without serving at least seven years as an apprentice and

BELOW Apprenticeship indentures included strict conditions about how the apprentice should behave.

until reaching the age of 24. In 1768, this was reduced to 21, and the statute remained in force until 1814, although by that time enforcement of it had become rather lax. The 1563 legislation also applied only to occupations then in existence. As other trades started, the requirement that practitioners should serve an apprenticeship in full was not enforced in many cases.

If the master could not complete the full term of training, arrangements were usually made to find another master to complete the apprenticeship. This was known as "turning over".

There were three distinct kinds of apprenticeship:
- voluntary apprenticeship, where the child was placed by its parents
- Poor Law apprenticeship, where parish authorities placed a child in the master's care
- apprenticeship to a guild or livery company of a town or city

Voluntary apprenticeship

This was a private arrangement, usually made by parents on behalf of their child. They paid someone a fee to cover the cost of tuition as well as the

apprentice's keep while he or she was learning. Both parties signed a legal document called an indenture, which had two parts. One part was kept by the parents and the other by the master.

If children were apprenticed to their father, mother or another relative, there was only a token fee.

Between 1710 and 1808, apprenticeship premiums over 1s were taxed. The records, which actually finish in 1811, are in The National Archives (TNA). Until around 1752 they contain the parents' or guardian's names. There are indexes up to 1774 to both masters and apprentices in TNA, the Guildhall Library and the Society of Genealogists' library. Poor Law apprenticeships were exempt, so will not appear here, nor will the apprenticeship of a child to a father.

Poor Law apprenticeship

It was the responsibility of the overseer of the poor for each parish to provide for orphans and those children whose parents were too impoverished to care for them. The 1601 Poor Relief Act allowed parish officers, with the consent of Justices of the Peace (JPs), to bind a child under the age of 14 to a master (either a man or woman). This was not a proper apprenticeship, and was called an "apprenticeship binding". Often these hapless children were simply used as unpaid labour rather than being taught a skill.

In 1696, it became compulsory to take apprentices in this way, and masters were selected in rotation or chosen by ballot. Apprenticeship bindings lasted until 1834. Since 1662, serving a full term of apprenticeship had given settlement rights in a parish, and so officials tried to find masters outside their own parish, in order to evade potential responsibility for the apprentice and any dependants. Records

relating to Poor Law apprentices will be found in parish records in the CRO. The SoG has a large collection of original indentures made between 1641 and 1888, including many Poor Law apprenticeships.

There were also local charities that paid for the apprenticeship of poor children, although as time went on better-off parents sometimes managed to get their sons and daughters placed in good trades through this route. These records will be found in the CRO.

Guild apprenticeship

Members of guilds were responsible for teaching apprentices their various trades and crafts. Completing a guild apprenticeship brought all kinds of privileges, so a high premium could be charged for taking one. A record of these premiums appear in TNA's tax records, as well as in the records of the guilds themselves, which are usually in the CRO.

Guild records will also contain information about disputes over apprenticeships and the turning over of an apprentice from one master to another. Sometimes this was due to the inability of a master to continue in business, but in other cases children simply proved to have no aptitude for or interest in a craft, and so started again in a different trade or skill.

Quarter sessions papers contain many examples of apprentices petitioning to be released from their indentures because their master was either not teaching them his or her craft or ill-treating them. Some apprentices did not go to the trouble of legal proceedings: they just ran away, and advertisements for their return may be found in local newspapers. Anyone employing such a runaway was liable to prosecution. Newspapers may also contain reports of legal proceedings. Masters

also went to law to cancel the indenture of an unsatisfactory apprentice.

APPRENTICESHIPS IN THE 19TH AND 20TH CENTURIES

The strict controls exercised over apprentices started to loosen in the mid-18th century. Many people did not complete their full term but still practised a trade.

In the 19th century, with the growth of large companies, apprentices were increasingly taken on by businesses, such as shipbuilders, gas companies, and motor manufacturers.

Surviving records of indentures from the 19th and 20th centuries will be found either in company archives (many deposited with CROs) or among private family papers.

RESEARCHING APPRENTICESHIP RECORDS

Completing an apprenticeship was one of the ways after 1662 in which to gain settlement in a parish, and so settlement examinations will always say whether an apprenticeship was started and if it was completed, and will give the name and parish of the master.

The dates of the beginning and end of an apprenticeship will give clues to the person's age: the standard term was seven years, ending at the age of 21 (or 24 in the 16th and 17th centuries).

Directories and advertisements in newspapers may help to locate where an ancestor served as an apprentice.

FURTHER HELP

TNA fact sheet *Apprentices and masters*
Raymond, Stuart A. *My Ancestor was an Apprentice* (SoG)
Some guild records, including lists of apprenticeships, have been published

---

Guilds and freemen

The guilds of cities and towns began in the Middle Ages. They were originally made up of reputable merchants, tradesmen and craftsmen who organized themselves into groups to maintain occupational standards and agree prices. They also arranged many welfare services for their members, such as insurance, burial clubs and financial support for widows and orphans of members.

Someone who had successfully completed an apprenticeship to a member of one of the guilds became a freeman, which usually gave the right to vote in local elections.

BECOMING A FREEMAN

At the end of his or her guild apprenticeship, the aspiring guild member produced an example of the skills that had been learned. This was often a miniature article, such as a piece of furniture, and was called the "masterpiece". If this masterpiece was considered satisfactory, the person paid a fee to be enrolled into the guild as a freeman and could practise his or, much more rarely, her trade.

Most men then became journeymen. This name is not connected to the fact that they travelled around, which they often did, but comes from the fact that they were paid by the day. (It comes from the French word *journée*.) They worked on a casual basis until they had the means to set up their own businesses, hire other workers and take on their own apprentices. The more prudent ones waited until they found somewhere that needed their skills before settling down and starting a family.

There were three other ways of becoming a freeman:

- by redemption or fine, i.e. paying to join a guild or livery company when you had not completed an apprenticeship in its trade or craft
- by patrimony, if your father was a freeman at the time of your birth. In some places, therefore, the freedom of a guild or borough could be inherited and passed down through the generations, although this usually applied only to eldest sons. This inherited freedom still operates in some of the ancient boroughs,

so you may find that you or your eldest son are entitled to become a freeman.

- by marrying a freeman's widow or daughter (this was only practised in some guilds)

These different methods meant that a man might have a different trade from that of the guild he entered.

If someone was expelled from a guild, he would not be allowed to trade within the radius of the city or town. This is where the expression "sent to Coventry" may have originated.

Freemen had certain rights granted to them by the city or town:

- to take apprentices
- to trade
- to vote for officials such as the Mayor and Aldermen, and also in national elections.

In addition, freemen were responsible for local government functions, such as the running of schools and care of the poor, as well as the administration of both civil and criminal law within their borough, including inquests. Many guilds supported local charities and educational establishments.

ABOVE The guilds and livery companies of the City of London have their own crests (from left to right: the Mercers, Merchant Tailors, Grocers and Ironmongers), which may appear on heirlooms and provide the family historian with clues about an ancestor's membership.

CITY OF LONDON GUILDS

Outside London there was usually a single guild to which all traders and craftsmen belonged, whatever their business. In the City of London, however, there were different livery companies and guilds, which originally had their basis in specific occupations. (The livery companies are chartered companies that originated from the craft guilds.) There are 102 companies, of which 77 are ancient and 25 modern. Before about 1700, people tended to belong to the same company as their trade. From 1750, the other methods of gaining the freedom of the City became more common. The cost of apprenticeship to a citizen of London meant that skilled people who could not afford to become a freeman tended to live in the parishes around the Square Mile.

CITY OF LONDON BROKERS

Commodity brokers who wanted to trade in the City of London had to be freemen (until 1856) and be licensed by the City authorities (until 1886), although some evaded being licensed from the 19th century onwards. They were issued with a medal to prove their credentials. The numbers of Jews and other aliens were strictly limited. Between 1738 and 1830, Jews were not admitted to the freedom of the City, but twelve were allowed to become brokers.

KING'S/QUEEN'S FREEMEN

Between 1784 and 1873, discharged servicemen and their wives and children had the right to trade in any town in the British Isles. They were called King's/Queen's Freemen, and received a certificate. Relatively few seem to have taken advantage of this, because, from the beginning of the 19th century, strict control started to decline. Fewer and fewer men chose to pay the

ABOVE The Stock Exchange was set up in 1760 by a group of men thrown out of the Royal Exchange for rowdy behaviour. By Victorian times, it was a respectable place to work.

costs of guild membership, especially if they had done their apprenticeship in a city or town but decided to set up in business elsewhere, so King's/Queen's Freemen had no special advantages.

HONORARY FREEMEN

City and borough councils could grant someone who had done their community some special service the title of honorary freeman.

RESEARCHING GUILD RECORDS

Electoral registers and poll books before about 1835 will list those who had the right to vote in local and national elections. They usually state how the individual was qualified to vote, including if they were freemen. If your City of London ancestor was a grocer, he may not have joined the Grocers' Company. The variety of ways of becoming a freeman means that he could also have belonged to any of the other companies.

Wills usually state whether a person was a member of a City of London livery company.

The archives of most of the City of London's livery companies and guilds are in the Guildhall Library, but a few remain with the companies themselves. There is a complete list of freemen between 1681 and 1915, which includes the guild to which they belonged. City of London apprenticeship records are in the process of being published. The guild records of many provincial cities and boroughs have been published, at least up to 1800.

FURTHER HELP

LMA Information Leaflet Number 14: City Freedom Archives
LMA Information Leaflet Number 15: Sworn Brokers Archives
LMA Information Leaflet Number 16: Searching for members or those apprenticed to members of City of London livery companies www.cityoflondon.gov.uk
Aldous, Vivienne E. *My Ancestors Were Freemen of the City of London* (SoG)
Family and local history societies have compiled lists of freemen. Try the Genfair catalogue to see what has been published.

The professions

The British practice of leaving land and money to the eldest son meant that the other children had to make their own way in the world. Within the upper classes, there was sometimes enough money in the family to ensure that younger sons didn't have to do anything so vulgar as work, and the lower middle classes had businesses or trades to pass on to their sons, but there were many families where profitable occupations had to be found for their sons. (The daughters were expected to marry well.) Some purchased commissions as Army officers or went into the Navy; others became clergymen, lawyers or perhaps doctors but not, until the late 19th century, surgeons, who were not held in such high respect.

THE CHURCH

Clergymen of the Church of England usually went to university, then, having obtained their degree, were appointed to a parish, either as the incumbent or as a curate. Many parishes, or livings, were in the gift of the bishop of a diocese or an individual, such as a lord of the manor. In the 18th century, it was common for a clergyman to have more than one living: he would pay a curate to look after the parishioners of the less glamorous parish, or parishes, and live elsewhere.

There were often complaints about clergymen neglecting their duties or committing other sins; these are found in the records of the Church courts in either the DRO or CRO. From 1792, all clergymen and preachers had to be licensed by the bishop, who also issued licences for a number of other matters,

ABOVE George Whitefield, one of the founders of Methodism, joined the society while at Oxford in 1735 before it broke away from the Church of England.

such as holding more than one living, or engaging in a trade. Not all clergymen became the incumbent of a parish: some became chaplains, others missionaries. Information about chaplains will be found among surviving papers of the organizations they served. There were a number of missionary societies linked to different denominations. Since they depended on subscriptions and voluntary contributions, they usually produced annual reports, which contain information about individuals' activities.

The Clergy List, published from 1841, lists the names of all the Anglican clergy and gives details of their livings, including when they were appointed, how much each living was worth per annum and who was the patron. From 1858 this list was taken over by a man called Crockford, and it continues as Crockford's Clerical Directory to the present day. There are other sources of information: most dioceses issued publications listing the personnel in them, and DROs and CROs may hold ordination papers for individual clergy, containing letters of recommendation, references and other useful documents.

Nonconformist clergy

After the restoration of Charles II in 1660, Nonconformist clergy faced official persecution. From 1672, they had to be licensed, but it was not until the 1689 Toleration Act that they and their congregations had complete freedom of worship.

Nonconformist clergy tended to come from a lower social class than Anglican clergy, and, as they did not have parish tithes to support them, they depended on what their congregation could give them and what they could earn themselves. Most, therefore, had another occupation. Surviving records will be found in the denomination's archives. From the mid-19th century, most produced both magazines and directories, which contain obituaries and other biographical material on ministers.

Researching clerical records

Look first at the lists of Oxbridge alumni, which contain biographical details. From there, you can go on to the records of the organizations or places where your ancestor(s) worked.

If your ancestor isn't an Oxbridge graduate, look at the records of Nonconformist colleges in the 19th century, or records of licences.

THE LAW

There was, and still is, a distinction between solicitors (known as attorneys until 1875) and barristers. Only the latter could appear in court to plead for their clients. Attorneys conducted legal business, such as drawing up marriage settlements and wills or dealing with property matters. Some also dealt with other estate business, such

as collecting rents, and were involved with manorial courts. Attorneys could also carry out their clients' business in those courts to which they were admitted to practise.

Qualifying for the law

People wanting to become barristers mainly went to university, either Oxford or Cambridge, and then to the Inns of Court in London, where they had to remain for a certain period of time before qualifying. An examination was introduced in 1853. Those wanting to become solicitors might also go to university, but the majority were apprenticed. The period of apprenticeship was fixed at five years in 1728.

Researching legal records

Most of the admission registers of the Inns of Court have been published. Surviving records that have not appeared in print are still with the individual Inns, apart from those of Clement's Inn, which are held by TNA. It's also worth checking the registers of the chapels attached to the inns: barristers were sometimes married or had children baptized there.

TNA holds records of attorneys admitted to the various courts: Common Pleas, King's/Queen's Bench,

FURTHER HELP

Brooks, Brian & Herber, Mark *My Ancestor was a Lawyer* (SoG)
TNA factsheets covering attorneys, barristers and lawyers
Towey, Peter *My Ancestor was an Anglican Clergyman* (SoG)

Exchequer, Equity, Chancery, Bankruptcy, the Palatinate Courts, High Court of Admiralty and the Prerogative Court of Canterbury. Lawyers practising in the last two courts were called "proctors". An oath had to be sworn before they could be admitted, which effectively disbarred Catholics from practising in these courts before 1791. Judges also had to take an oath.

The Law List, containing attorneys, was published from 1780, and the Law Society was founded in 1828. The society also holds records relating to their members dating back, in some cases, to 1790. A tax on apprenticeships 1710–1811 means attorneys appear in these records too.

Some lawyers completed their training but did not practise, so if you find an ancestor in the records of the Inns of Court or apprenticeship records, don't assume that he became a lawyer. An education in the law was regarded as good preparation for life.

LEFT Judges' wigs and gowns date from the late 17th century, when they were everyday wear.

ABOVE Calling in a doctor was expensive, and before the mid-19th century he had few effective remedies for illness.

ABOVE Apothecaries dispensed medicines and offered advice to those too poor to pay for a doctor.

MEDICINE

Since the medical profession deals with life and death, it has, for obvious reasons, been strictly regulated. Before the 19th century, when there were considerable advances in both medical science and public health, the profession was not highly specialized. Women were largely responsible for their families' wellbeing and any nursing that needed to be done. Calling in a doctor might be expensive and, in many cases, there was little that he could do. Some of the drugs in common use, like mercury, might be almost as harmful to the patient as the diseases they were meant to cure. Many people relied on folk medicine, like wrapping an old sock or stocking around the neck to cure a sore throat, or went to people who had a reputation for herbal medicines (but no formal qualification or licence).

Physicians and surgeons

From medieval times, there was a sharp distinction between physicians and surgeons. Before anaesthetics made invasive surgery possible, only minor operations, blood letting and amputations could be carried out, and their familiarity with razors meant that barbers carried out these operations. In London, surgeons belonged to the same company as barbers until 1745, when a separate Company of Surgeons was established. Training was by apprenticeship.

Surgery was considered only one step up from butchery, so the men who went into this branch of medicine were (and still are) called "Mr", rather than "Doctor". Medical men who went to sea were almost invariably surgeons: the ability to carry out amputations was vital in battle. The Royal College of Surgeons was founded in 1801.

Physicians treated all illnesses not requiring surgery: indeed, some prided themselves on not touching their patients at all. Before the late 18th century, they were apprenticed, but increasingly went to university, especially in Scotland. Lists of university graduates have been published. From 1512, all medical men practising in London had to be licensed by the Bishop of London.

Apothecaries

Apothecaries, who dispensed drugs and medicines, and chemists and druggists, who made them, came into the medical profession through apprenticeship. Both doctors and surgeons might also have training as apothecaries. From 1815, they had to be licensed by the Society of Apothecaries, whose records are in the Guildhall Library.

Dentists

In early years, dentistry consisted of little more than extracting teeth. Any strong person could set himself, or more rarely herself, up as a tooth-puller. The first dental hospital, which also carried out training, was founded in London in 1858.

Nurses and midwives

Women have been involved in caring for the sick since before records began. From medieval times, many orders of nuns were involved in this work. After the dissolution of the monasteries, a few hospitals remained, and women worked in them, but they were rarely those who had gone into nursing because of a religious vocation. Most were elderly widows, for whom the alternative was starvation, and they were paid a pittance for their work. Workhouses and parish infirmaries usually employed a matron and occasionally other women, often one of the paupers in the workhouse, to care for the sick.

Hospitals were very unhygienic and dangerous places to stay in, so most people preferred to be cared for at home and might hire nurses to look after them there, especially after childbirth. There was no recognized training for nurses, and those who undertook such work had the unwelcome reputation of being drunken, slovenly and incompetent.

Florence Nightingale transformed both the image and the training of nurses. After her experiences in Scutari during the Crimean War, she came back to Britain determined to make nursing a skilled and respectable profession. The first training school for nurses was set up at St Thomas's Hospital in London in 1860. State registration of nurses began in 1919.

Researching records of medical practitioners

Since 1845, an annual directory of practitioners has been published as the *British Medical Directory*, and this is the best starting point for the family historian looking for medics. Dentists were included from 1886. Local and trade directories list medical practitioners before and after these dates.

FURTHER HELP

TNA factsheets as follows:
Health
Hospitals
Patients, doctors and nurses
Higgs, Michelle *Tracing Your Medical Ancestors* (Pen & Sword)

Records of apprenticeships can be found in TNA for 1710–1811.

Before the mid-18th century, physicians, surgeons and midwives had to be licensed by the bishop of their diocese, because they might have to baptize a newborn child in danger of dying. Records will be found in Diocesan Record Offices (DROs) or CROs.

The United Kingdom Central Council for Nursing, Midwifery and Health Visiting (UKCC) holds a list of registered practitioners, but this has only their date of registration. To go further, you need to know in which hospital your ancestor trained. Photographs may help, as hospitals had their own, distinctive uniforms. Records relating to military and naval nurses will be in TNA.

ABOVE Until the 20th century, most women gave birth at home.

RIGHT Florence Nightingale's efforts made the nursing profession respectable.

Other occupations

It would, of course, be impossible to give information about every job that every person in everyone's ancestry might have done. This section covers some of the occupations for which good records exist, because the people who did them were public servants.

STARTING THE SEARCH

First you need to find out what your ancestor did, using sources such as:

- apprenticeship records
- BMD certificates
- burgess or freemen's rolls
- censuses

ABOVE **Domestic service employed a huge proportion of women before World War I.**

- directories
- newspapers
- quarter sessions (when licences were granted)
- wills

Before about 1830, occupations were not given for a large number of people. In rural areas, you can suspect that they were agricultural labourers (usually listed as "ag. labs." in records). Before the mid-19th century, more people lived in the countryside than towns, and farming employed many generally unskilled labourers.

Other unskilled or semi-skilled labour was required in the factories that were established by the Industrial Revolution, which started at the end of the 18th century. In industrial areas, those people whose occupation is not given are likely to be factory hands or general labourers.

While many jobs could be done in any part of the country, some areas had concentrations of particular trades, such as miners. Coal was mined in South Wales and in various places in the north of England and Scotland. Tin mining was a speciality of Cornwall, and lead of Derbyshire. Fishing was an important source of employment in coastal areas and along major rivers.

SERVANTS

Until the end of World War I, the majority of people spent some or the whole of their lives as servants. Even lower-middle-class people expected to employ at least one servant to help the mistress of the house, and on a large estate there might be a staff of up to a hundred. Some lived in; others came in on a daily basis.

The word "servant" covered a range of jobs. Farm servants were not necessarily domestic workers: they were unmarried men and women who lived on the premises. Once married, and living in a separate dwelling, the men were known as agricultural labourers. (Their wives invariably worked too, but on a casual basis as the demands of raising a family permitted.)

THE POLICE

In addition to the armed forces, there were other occupations that required the wearing of a uniform, of

ABOVE **The uniformed policeman became a familiar sight during the 19th century.**

which a photograph might help to identify an ancestor's job. Among these jobs was membership of the police force.

Before the early 19th century, law enforcement was largely the responsibility of individual parishes. They had a constable, whose policing duties extended to little beyond locking up apprehended criminals and ensuring their attendance at court. The constable was also charged with ensuring that market stall-holders and shopkeepers obeyed the trading laws. In towns and cities, watchmen, usually elderly men, might be hired to patrol the street at night to deter lawbreakers. There was very little in the way of detective work done – it was largely the person against whom a crime was perpetrated who had to bring the criminal to justice.

In London, the problems of crime were much more pressing than elsewhere. The magistrate Sir John Fielding set up the Bow Street Runners, who were paid constables. In 1829, the first police force was set up in London, covering an 11-km (7-mile) radius from Charing Cross but excluding the City of London.

ABOVE Miners, such as this Yorkshire pitman, played an important role in the creation of Britain's wealth through the Industrial Revolution.

Before World War II, many towns and boroughs might have had their own police force. Since then, they have been amalgamated into larger geographical units. In addition to those dealing with street crime, there are other divisions, such as forces policing ports, rivers, railways (including the London Underground) and airports.

Researching records relating to the police

The records of London's Metropolitan Police are in TNA. Other forces' records will be with the CRO or the relevant force's museum. Some may remain in the force's headquarters. The Police History Society covers all aspects of police history, and many individual forces have their own museums and societies whose members have published histories.

There are several publications of use to the family historian. *Hue and Cry*, published from the early 19th century, became the *Police Gazette* in 1828. Both listed army deserters, the names of criminals on the run who had absconded and unsolved crimes,

and they often included the names of the police officers in charge of cases. The *Police Service Advertiser* was published between 1866 and 1959. *The Police Review (and Parade Gossip)*, published from 1893, is indexed.

The Illustrated Police News (1864–1938) was a sensationalist magazine that described the more lurid crimes and court proceedings, and often included sketches of the policemen involved. In addition to these specialist magazines, both local and national newspapers reported in detail crimes and trials at which police officers gave evidence.

ABOVE Before mechanization, agricultural labour employed many unskilled workers.

FURTHER HELP

TNA factsheet *Master craftsmen and tradesmen*
Police History Society www.policehistorysociety.co.uk
Horn, Pamela *My Ancestor was in Service* (SoG)
Shearman, Anthony *My Ancestor was a Policeman* (SoG)
Wade, Stephen *Tracing Your Police Ancestors: A Guide for Family Historians* (Pen & Sword)

ABOVE The introduction of the penny post meant that even the less well off could keep in touch with their families.

FIREFIGHTERS

Early firefighters were either employees of the fire insurance companies or volunteers. The insurance companies employed firemen and porters (the latter carried out the salvage operation after a fire). Records relating to fire brigades are usually deposited in the CROs.

AWARDS FOR BRAVERY

Many of those in the above-mentioned uniformed services behaved heroically in the course of their duties and might have received recognition of this. There are various awards for particular services.

Ordinary people were also given awards for bravery. There are a number of organizations that might have issued some token, such as a medal or certificate. One of the main bodies involved in this is the Royal Humane Society, which was established in 1774, originally as a way of encouraging people to bring drowned bodies to two doctors who were interested in

researching resuscitation techniques. It grew into a charity that both employed rescuers stationed at places, such as rivers and lakes, where drowning was a danger, and gave awards for bravery. Some of its records date back to its founding, and it has a list of awards made from 1823 onwards. These have not been indexed, so the date of the event, which would have been covered in newspapers, is necessary to get further information.

THE POST OFFICE

In 1636, Charles I allowed the general public to use the royal mail services, and the Post Office was born. In 1840 the practice of requiring the sender, rather than the recipient, of a letter or package to pay began. An adhesive stamp, the first being the Penny Black, showed that the sum had been paid.

Although most of its records were destroyed in the Great Fire of London in 1666, the Post Office's archives include some records dating back to 1636. From 1719, many Post Office employees received pensions, and their

application forms are indexed. In addition to information about employees' appointments and careers, there are copies of union publications, company newsletters and magazines, and an extensive collection of photographs and artwork. Records relating to telegraph and telephone services are now with British Telecommunications, and these include telephone directories dating from 1880.

RAILWAYS

Originally the railway system in Britain consisted of individual private companies. In 1947, the whole railway system was nationalized, and the vast majority of surviving records of all the different companies were deposited in TNA or the Scottish Record Office (SRO), though a few may be in CROs. There are many books available on aspects of the railways and their history.

OTHER COMPANY ARCHIVES

Histories of many individual companies have been written and published, but they will usually mention only

ABOVE The vast amount of waste produced in cities needed an army of refuse collectors and cleaners, many of whom were women.

the higher echelons of employees. Archives may have been deposited in CROs, while others remain with the company. Many large organizations, including department stores and hotels, have their own archives. Among their records may be personnel details and company newsletters, which usually mention people's retirements and carry obituaries.

RESEARCHING ANCESTORS INVOLVED IN A PARTICULAR OCCUPATION

There are a large number of occupational indexes. Some are in the possession of individuals who have, through a personal interest, set them up; others are attached to specialist museums. Local historians may also have set up an index of everyone in their area of study, which will include the occupations of all the people there. It is quite difficult to find out where all these indexes are located, as many people have compiled them mainly for their own interest. Increasingly they can be found online.

The title and further information about companies, particular occupations and directories of those engaged in them can be found by typing an occupation into the search engine of the British Library's on-line catalogue. The book can then be ordered through your local library's service or, if this is impossible, read at the British Library or the nearest library that holds a copy, which your library should be able to discover for you.

More and more out-of-print books, including annual reports and histories of organizations, are now being put online. Google Books and Project Gutenberg are the main sites, but there are others.

It is worth remembering that every trade or occupation has its own associ-

ABOVE Working for a railway company was regarded as a prestigious job and brought a pension, which meant a secure old age.

ation and specialist magazine. Some professional societies, including the livery companies, date from medieval times, but from the 19th century onwards trade associations for other occupations were set up. Records of members may still be with the relevant association; if not, the association should be able to tell you where they are now deposited.

Many of the skills learned by people in the past no longer exist or have been replaced by machines. If you find that a reference to your ancestor's occupation is something you don't understand, and a dictionary does not contain it, try consulting a book such as the *Book of Trades or Library of Useful Arts* (pub. 1811–18 and reprinted by Wiltshire Family History Society), which helpfully describes pre-19th-century occupations, or Colin Waters' *A Dictionary of Old Trades, Occupations and Titles*.

FURTHER HELP

BT Group Archives, Third Floor, Holborn Telephone Exchange, 268–270 High Holborn, London WC1V 7EE www.btlp.com

The Directory of British Associations and Associations in Ireland (CRD Research) and other similar directories publish contact details of associations in existence today and usually give the date of foundation.

Culling, Joyce *An Introduction to ... Occupations* (FHP)

Drummond, Di *Tracing Your Railway Ancestors: A Guide For Family Historians* (Pen & Sword)

Hardy, Frank *My Ancestor Was a Railway Worker* (SoG)

Hawkings, David T. *Railway Ancestors: A guide to the staff records of the railway companies of England and Wales 1822–1947* (The History Press)

Torrance, D. Richard *Scottish Trades and Professions: A Selected Bibliography* (SAFHS)

Licences

A number of occupations required the practitioner to have a licence. Sometimes it was a matter of ensuring competence, as in the case of game-keepers. In other instances, such as printers, it was to ensure that laws were not broken.

LEFT Anyone selling alcohol needed a licence, which could be withdrawn if customers became too rowdy.

VICTUALLERS

There can be very few families who do not have someone connected with the manufacture or sale of alcohol in their ancestry. (In some places, every third house was licensed to brew or sell alcohol, in the times when water was too dangerous to drink.) The Crown also made money by selling licences to import and sell wine and spirits.

Different regulations applied to ale-houses, taverns and inns. An alehouse was usually a small establishment where ale, beer or sometimes cider was made on the premises and sold to customers. Often this was a single person working from his or her own home. Taverns, which were in towns, boroughs or cities, offered wine as well as ale and might also have sold spirits. Inns sold alcoholic drinks and had rooms where travellers could stay.

The first law regulating the sale of alcohol was passed in 1553. Licences to sell alcohol had to be granted by JPs, which remains the case today. People who wanted to provide entertainment as well as sell alcohol on their premises needed a licence from 1752, and if they also wanted to hire out horses they had to get a separate licence from 1784.

In 1828, the laws were revised and different types of licences to sell beer, wine and spirits on and off premises

were granted. From 1830, those selling only beer and cider could get a licence from the local excise office rather than in court.

Locating records of alcohol-related licences

The National Archives holds records relating to licences to sell wine in the 16th and 17th centuries, and some licences for this period are also found in quarter sessions held in CROs. From the 18th century, matters to do with licences - both the granting of them and cases involving illegal sales - were dealt with at petty and quarter sessions. Recent records relating to licences may still be with the magistrates' courts that granted them.

GAMEKEEPERS

Between 1710 and the middle of the 20th century, the men who looked after the game birds on a country estate were supposed to be registered at the local quarter sessions, though it seems that this was not always observed. Court records may also contain legal proceedings relating to

poachers apprehended by gamekeepers. Estate records mentioning gamekeepers may remain with the owner or may have been deposited in CROs or other repositories. Local directories may also list gamekeepers in their area.

COACHMEN AND DRIVERS

Coachmen in general did not have to have a licence or be registered anywhere, but hackney coachmen, the taxi-drivers of the 19th and early 20th century, did have to be licensed. Records of these licences, which do not include the licences themselves, are in TNA. Sometimes hackney coachmen gave the number of their licence in census returns.

London taxi-drivers are now licensed by the Public Carriage Office, but records of individual cabbies are destroyed six years after their death or

FURTHER HELP

Gibson, Jeremy *Victuallers' Licences: Records for Family and Local Historian* (FHP)
Fowler, Simon *Researching Brewery and Publican Ancestors* (FHP)

retirement. Other local authorities generally license taxi-drivers in their own area, and the survival of records depends on their policies.

From 1903, drivers of motor vehicles, including motorcycles, had to have a licence issued by the local authorities, so surviving records will be in CROs.

PAWNBROKERS AND CHIMNEYSWEEPS

From 1786, pawnbrokers in all parts of the country had to have annual revenue licences. Records before the Pawnbrokers' Act of 1872 are sparse, but after this date there are some records in CROs, since the licence was dependent on a certificate granted by a magistrate. Chimney sweeps were given similar certificates after 1875.

TRAVELLING SALESPEOPLE

Itinerant sellers of goods had to be licensed by a magistrate from 1698 to 1772. They had to wear a badge showing that they were licensed, and so were sometimes called "badgers". These records will be in the CRO, and there are also lists of licences granted in TNA among the Exchequer records. There was a fine line between sellers of some goods, such as matches, and beggars. From 1531, beggars had to be licensed by JPs or mayors.

DROVERS

Before railways and motorized transport, the only way to get cattle and other animals, such as sheep, pigs and even geese, to market was to drive them there. Most, of course, went to the nearest market town, but others were taken much longer distances to cities, especially London. The men engaged in this trade were known as drovers, and they, like other itinerants, were licensed.

BARGEES AND RIVER SAILORS

Boats had always been used to transport goods around Britain's coastline and along the navigable rivers inland. The first canals were constructed in the late 18th century by private companies. There were no common agreements between them about the width and depth of these waterways, so barges could be used only on particular canals, which was restrictive.

Between 1795 and 1871, owners of barges had to be licensed. Records of christenings, marriages and burials (CMBs) of bargees, river sailors and their families should be found in the parishes along the route of canals. Some families actually lived on their barges, while others had a home on land instead.

The 1861 census uniquely required additional details about ships in port to be included, and, since this would include river and canal boats delivering or collecting goods to or from ports, respectively, it is a useful source of information. There is an index to ships' names in TNA. In 1877, an Act required registers of canal boats to be kept, and those that survive are usually in CROs.

PRINTERS AND PUBLISHERS

The government has always worried about what is published, especially if it criticizes them, but also if it contains material defined as seditious, blasphemous or obscene. Since 1834, all printed material has had to contain the name and address of the printer. Between 1799 and 1869, the owners of printing presses had to be licensed.

GUN OWNERS

Not surprisingly, a strict eye was kept on those who owned guns (a situation that has not changed today), and the manufacturers of guns were also carefully regulated. Initially most gunsmiths worked in and around the City of London and belonged to one of the livery companies there. After the Civil War, the Midlands, especially Birmingham, became another centre of arms manufacture. The government was a major customer, and employed some gunsmiths through the Board of Ordnance, whose records are in TNA. The arms they made had to be tested in proof houses, which still exist. The one in Whitechapel, East London, dates back to 1675.

ABOVE Before the growth of railways and motor vehicles, the waterways were an important form of transport. Barge owners needed a licence.

Elections, poll books and electoral registers

Until the 20th century, the majority of people did not have the vote, which usually depended on owning property as a qualification.

PARLIAMENTARY ELECTIONS
Before the 19th century, Members of Parliament were returned for three types of constituency: counties, boroughs (burghs in Scotland) and the universities of Oxford and Cambridge.

County MPs
The franchise was largely based on property qualifications. Before 1832, the vote was restricted to those who possessed land or a house worth 40s or more in annual rent.

ABOVE Only a small section of the population could vote, and they cast their ballots in public until 1872. Allegations of bribery and vote-rigging were common.

Borough franchises
Only those towns that had an ancient charter were boroughs. This is why many of the northern and Midlands towns that grew out of the Industrial Revolution had no individual MPs but were included in the county elections until after the 1832 Reform Act.

The vote in these boroughs depended on local customs. In some, all freemen had the franchise but in others, it was only those who were resident there that qualified. In some boroughs, ratepayers could vote. The lists of people entitled to vote in boroughs are called burgess or freemen's rolls.

The City of London
All the Acts that gradually eroded the rights of freemen in boroughs to elect their own MPs and officials have always excluded the City of London, where a system of government, relatively unchanged since medieval times, still operates.

The right to vote

Until the 20th century, the majority of people did not have the right to vote. At various times, certain people were not allowed to vote in parliamentary elections:

- women (until 1918, and even then there were certain restrictions)
- peers of the realm (though peeresses could vote between 1918 and 1963)
- those under 21

- lunatics
- sentenced criminals in prison
- aliens who had not been naturalized
- those in receipt of public alms, i.e. those receiving outdoor relief (money given to poor people not living in a workhouse) or those living in parish workhouses
- anyone convicted of bribery at an election
- those not included in an

electoral register (after 1832, when they were introduced)

Certain occupational groups were also excluded:
- serving policemen (before 1887)
- postmasters (until 1918)
- customs and excise men (until 1918)

Conscientious objectors in World War I were also forbidden to vote in the 1918 and 1923 parliamentary elections.

Significant dates in the history of the franchise in England and Wales

1429 All men over the age of 21 who held land or property with a rental value of 40s or more per annum in a county, and were resident there, could vote in county elections.

1774 Men no longer needed to be resident in the county where their property was situated in order to vote.

1832 Reform Act revised constituencies and extended the county franchise to tenants of land worth between £2 and £5 per annum (p.a.); to those paying more than £50 p.a. in rent; and to those with a long lease on land worth more than £10 p.a. All the varied qualifications in the borough franchises were standardized to those who had property with a ratable value of more than £10 p.a. All voters had to have paid their rates and taxes. This Act also introduced electoral registers.

1867 Representation of the People Act gave the vote to all men paying £10 or more p.a. for housing in towns (but not in rural areas), reduced the property value in counties to £5 and extended the franchise to all men paying £50 or more per year in rent for a building or land. The right afforded to Oxford and Cambridge to elect their own MP was extended to the University of London.

1869 Municipal Franchise Act gave unmarried women who paid rates the right to vote for certain local officials.

1870 Electoral rights of unmarried women ratepayers extended to school boards.

1872 Secret ballot introduced.

1888 County Electors Act allowed women with property qualifications to elect county councillors.

1894 Married women allowed to vote for local officials on the same basis as unmarried women.

1918 Women over 30 allowed to vote in national elections if either a householder or married to a householder.

1928 All men and women over the age of 21 given the vote.

1971 Age of majority (and therefore the right to vote) reduced from 21 to 18.

University seats

Oxford and Cambridge returned two MPs each. They were elected by the universities' legislative assemblies.

POLL BOOKS

In 1696, the sheriff of a county was given responsibility for compiling a list of all those who voted in a county election and for whom they cast their vote. This was to be made available to anyone who wanted to consult it. In 1843, a similar Act was passed relating to borough elections, but, unfortunately, most of these manuscript documents have been destroyed.

The poll was not secret before 1872, and poll books were published. They often include an account of the electoral campaign, though they are not always completely accurate. There is also no standard format. People who were not able to vote, for example those whose religion meant that they could not take the oath of allegiance, might or might not be listed. The candidate's political party might not be recorded, so you will have to look at a parliamentary history book to find out whether he was a Whig or a Tory. It is a good idea for family historians to investigate the policies of the individuals for whom their ancestors voted.

Researching poll books and electoral registers

These usually state individuals' addresses, occupations and qualifications for voting, which will give you further avenues to explore.

After 1774, when voters no longer had to be resident in the counties where they had property, land tax records were often used to prove their qualifications. Copies made of these might be found among quarter sessions records in CROs.

If you find that your ancestor appears in one poll book or electoral register but not the one before, don't automatically assume that he had only recently moved into the county. Check the date to see whether the franchise qualifications had changed in that time, as new legislation might have brought him into the electorate. In a borough, for example, he might have only recently become a freeman, either by completing his apprenticeship or by one of the other ways of gaining entry to a guild.

FURTHER HELP

Gibson, Jeremy and Rogers, Colin
Poll Books c.1696–1872: A Directory to Holdings in Great Britain [FHP]
Gibson, Jeremy and Rogers, Colin
Electoral Registers Since 1832 and Burgess Rolls: A Directory to Holdings in Great Britain [FHP]
In addition, there are a number of books about individual boroughs, counties and elections, which are listed in the Gibson Guides.

Trade unions and friendly societies

The government has always been highly suspicious of working men gathering together. At the end of the 18th century, the ruling class was afraid of revolution – a fear that the French Revolution largely confirmed – and it is true that many of the "corresponding societies" set up at about that time, ostensibly for social reasons and to discuss current affairs, did want changes in society. The two types of organization had much in common, especially in the early days: trade unions concentrated on pay and working conditions, while friendly societies concerned themselves with benefits for the unemployed and sick.

Another kind of revolution, the Industrial Revolution, began in this period, and changed the way people had previously worked. The scope for exploitation was now much greater, and workers realized the benefits of concerted action. The government responded with a series of laws against "combinations" – both trade unions and friendly societies.

TRADE UNIONS

From the mid-19th century, the government began to accept the right of people to form unions to negotiate with employers. Some unions were highly specialized, while others had a more general membership.

Throughout the 19th and 20th centuries, the number of unions grew. In many industries, membership became mandatory – the so-called "closed shop". Those who refused to join or who were rejected or expelled could not work in a particular company or occupation. This situation lasted until

the last quarter of the 20th century, so if you have ancestors in certain occupations, they will have been members of the relevant union. The Trades Union Congress (TUC), founded in 1920, is an association to which the majority of individual unions belong. Unions were an important factor in the founding, growth and development of the Labour Party.

Researching trade union records

The TUC Library Collections holds books and documents relating to the trade union movement. These largely relate to its history, but active and prominent members of unions may also appear in them. Its own archive holds records relating to the development of the TUC itself. Individual unions' records may still be with the

ABOVE Members of the Ancient Order of Foresters carry tools of agricultural trades.

LEFT Women were expected to support their menfolk when they went on strike.

union itself or may have been deposited in a separate archive, often within a university.

FRIENDLY SOCIETIES

Before the 20th century, illness and unemployment meant penury for not only the average working man but also his family. The workhouse was a grim experience, and, although there were charities to help, not everyone qualified for their assistance. To avoid the threat of the workhouse, groups of people would get together and pay into a fund designed to assist any of their number in financial trouble. Such benevolent and fraternal associations did, however, run the risk of being seen as a cover for political subversion. In 1793, the Friendly Societies Act regularized their position by requiring such clubs to draw up a set of rules and get themselves approved by local JPs, but this did not prevent official suspicion of their activities.

The major friendly societies were the Ancient Order of Foresters and the Independent Order of Oddfellows, but there were a number of other, smaller, ones. Individual branches were called "courts" in the Foresters and "lodges" in the Oddfellows, and, at the beginning, their members usually met at a local inn. Each member, who had to live within walking distance of the inn, received a certificate, which may survive in family papers. The courts or lodges retained the services of a medical man to provide treatment for its members. Those who were ill received sick pay, and a lump sum was paid to their families on death. As the trade union movement gathered strength, the membership of friendly societies declined.

Initially the Oddfellows met in public houses, but, during the mid-19th century, as the temperance move-

ABOVE By the 20th century, the trade unions had become a powerful political force, as well as supporting their members in times of unemployment.

ment grew, lodges began to build their own halls to keep their members away from the demon drink. The Oddfellows had a system whereby members could be issued with a document to allow them to stay overnight in any Oddfellows Hall. This was of great use to members looking for work. Emigrants took the principles of the society overseas, and Oddfellows lodges were founded in America and the Commonwealth. The American soci-

ety (which split from the British organization in 1834) founded lodges in many European countries.

Researching friendly society records

Surviving records may be with local branches, in record offices or with the individual societies' archives. There were also annual published accounts, which often included the names of officials and of members who had left or died in the preceding year.

FURTHER HELP

Foresters Heritage Trust,
  29-33 Shirley Road, Southampton
  SO15 2FE
  www.aoforestersheritage.com
Independent Order of Odd Fellows,
  Oddfellows House,
  40 Fountain Street,
  Manchester M2 2AB
  www.oddfellowsco.uk
Logan, Roger *An Introduction to Friendly Society Records* (FHP)
People's History Museum, Left Bank,
  Manchester M3 3ER houses the
  Labour History Archive and Study
  Centre (LHASC).
  www.phm.org.uk

TUC Archive, Modern Records
  Centre, University of Warwick
  Coventry CV4 7AL
  www.modernrecords.warwick.ac.uk
TUC Library Collections, Holloway
  Road Learning Centre,
  236-250 Holloway Road,
  London N7 6PP
  www.londonmet.ac.uk
Register of Friendly Societies
  www.mutuals.fsa.gov.uk
TNA holds records related to the
  register of Friendly Societies from
  c.1784-1999 and there is a fact sheet
  available.

For Crown and Country

There can be very few people who do not have an ancestor who was a member of the armed forces. As a major power, Britain was almost constantly at war with European nations until the mid-19th century and needed military personnel to defend and maintain its empire during the following one hundred years.

Members of the armed forces

The creation and maintenance of the British Empire needed considerable numbers of armed personnel. They were also called on to keep order at home before the advent of police forces from the mid-19th century.

SERVICEMEN AND WOMEN

To research service personnel, you need to think about what could have happened to a serviceman or woman. Every stage of his, or her, career would have generated records. The National Archives (TNA) has detailed leaflets giving the class marks of surviving records for the three branches of the services of all the events listed below, and more:

- joining up, either on a voluntary basis or through conscription
- training
- transferring from one unit to another
- wages
- commissions and promotion
- being awarded a medal or other distinction
- being taken prisoner
- dying in battle or while serving
- deserting
- getting court-martialled
- being discharged from the service
- pensions for those who survived
- widows', children's and dependants' pensions
- war memorials and graves

There was always a sharp distinction between officers and other ranks, and their records are generally kept

separately. Promotions of officers were published in the *London Gazette*, and lists of officers in the three services were published as the Army List, the Navy List and the Air Force List. The family historian must do more research work to find out about those lower down the hierarchy.

In addition to the soldiers, sailors and airmen, the armed forces needed support staff, and you may find your ancestors among them. They could be medical personnel, chaplains, spies or government employees of the Board of Ordnance, which was responsible for weapons, ammunition and stores. This division employed craftsmen, such as carpenters or smiths. Unfortunately, there are no records specifically relating to the craftsmen and others who supplied goods to the forces (though their names may appear in account books), because they were not directly employed by the government.

The East India Company had its own army and naval officers until 1858, when the company was wound up, so if you don't find a military or naval ancestor in the regular forces,

LEFT Recruiting Sergeants at Westminster in 1877 wait for potential recruits.

consider searching the East India Company records.

Any bookshop will reveal that military, naval and airforce history are subjects of enduring interest, and the family historian will find a great deal of background information in them. Some are, of course, academic tomes on the causes and tactics of a war, but others are more concerned with the individuals involved in campaigns and battles. One or more of these books may even include some research concerning your ancestor.

CONSCIENTIOUS OBJECTORS

In both World Wars, those who were opposed to fighting on moral, political or religious grounds, such as Quakers or Jehovah's Witnesses, had to go before a Military Service Tribunal to explain their reasons. Other people, who claimed that they were medically unfit or that their work was too valuable to stop, had to attend tribunals that were held locally. Special Tribunals were held for medical practitioners (including dentists) or vets who wanted to avoid conscription on the basis of their profession. There was also an Appeals Tribunal in almost every county for people who wanted to appeal against the local tribunal's decision. Some conscientious objectors were imprisoned and some were court-martialled.

Unfortunately, most of the government papers relating to World War I tribunals were destroyed in 1921, so TNA has only a few records relating to conscientious objectors. The minute book of the Central Tribunal, which dealt with appeals from the Special Tribunals, was kept, and the records of the Middlesex Appeals Tribunal and the Lothian and Peebles Local Tribunal were retained as samples. Not all other local tribunal records were destroyed, and those that did survive are now stored in either County Record Offices (CROs) or local record offices.

Some people avoided conscription in other ways – by fleeing to Ireland, by bribing officials or by taking drugs to make them appear medically unfit – and a few files relating to these people can be found in TNA.

COMMONWEALTH WAR GRAVES COMMISSION

Founded in 1917 as the Imperial War Graves Commission, this organization aims to care for the graves of members of the armed forces who died on or as a result of active service, and to commemorate those who have no known grave or who died as a result of enemy action. It maintains cemeteries all over the world and publishes lists of the dead buried there. Casualty lists were also published at the time in local newspapers and recorded on war memorials erected to commemorate those who died.

PRISONERS OF WAR

In earlier times, the majority of defeated enemies were usually put to death or enslaved. People of higher rank, however, might be ransomed.

By the mid-18th century, most captives were released after a period of imprisonment. TNA holds some lists

LEFT Temporary grave markers were made of wood until more permanent memorials could be erected.

BELOW World War I soldiers rest in the trenches.

of British POWs held in France and French POWs held in Britain during the French Revolution (1789–93) and Napoleonic Wars (1793–1815). The other 19th-century wars for which there are records relating to POWs in TNA are the Crimean War (1853–55) and the Boer War (1899–1902).

There are very few records in TNA relating to POWs from either of the World Wars: some records were destroyed by bombs, others, unfortunately, were destroyed as a result of official policy, and other records were passed to the International Commit-

tee of the Red Cross for safekeeping. The TNA leaflets listed on the following page give information about the records it holds.

INTERNMENT OF CIVILIANS DURING THE WORLD WARS

There was a great fear that nationals of countries against which Britain and her allies were fighting might be used as spies and saboteurs. Germans in World War I were rounded up (in some cases for their own protection) and interned in various places in Britain and Ireland. There was also a

Wars, campaigns and military actions involving British forces from 1538

1587–1603	War against Spain	1838–42	1st Afghan War	1914–18	World War I
1642–46	English Civil War	1839	Opium War	1919–21	Ireland
1652–54	1st Anglo-Dutch War		(against China)	1936–39	Palestine
1665–67	2nd Anglo-Dutch War	1843–48	1st Maori War	1939–45	World War II
1702–13	War of the Spanish		(in New Zealand)	1945–48	Campaign in Palestine
	Succession	1845–46	1st Sikh War	1946–47	Withdrawal from India
1739–42	War of Jenkins' Ear	1846	Maori insurrection	1948–60	Malayan Emergency
1740–48	War of the Austrian	1846–47	War against the Bantu	1950–53	Korean War
	Succession		(in South Africa)	1952–60	Mau-Mau Revolt
1753–63	Seven Years' War	1848–49	2nd Sikh War		(in Kenya)
1755–63	French and Indian War	1852–53	2nd Anglo-Burmese	1955–59	Campaign in Cyprus
	(in North America)		War	1956	Suez
1775–83	War of American	1853–56	Crimean War	1956–63	Northern Ireland
	Independence	1856–60	Anglo-Chinese War	1962	Brunei
1775–82	War with Marathas	1857–58	Indian Mutiny	1963–66	Borneo
	(in India)	1873–74	1st Ashanti War	1964–67	Aden
1779–83	Siege of Gibraltar	1875	3rd Anglo-Burmese	1969–	Northern Ireland
1793–1802	French Revolutionary		War	1982	Falklands Campaign
	War	1878–80	2nd Afghan War		
1803–15	Napoleonic Wars	1879	Zulu War	British forces have been, and still
1808–14	Peninsular War	1880–81	1st Boer War	are, involved as peace-keepers in a
1812–15	War in America	1882	Occupation of Egypt	number of places around the world.
1824–26	1st Anglo-Burmese	1896	2nd Ashanti War	The more recent the conflict, the
	War	1899–1902	2nd Boer War	easier it is to trace individuals.

---

camp on the Isle of Man, which was used again in World War II for Germans and Austrians, many of whom were refugees, and Italians, most of whom had arrived as economic migrants during the 1930s. The Manx Museum contains many records relating to those internees who were held on the Isle of Man.

Other camps were set up elsewhere, and a number of internees were sent to Canada and Australia. The initial panic had died down by 1941, and most of those held in camps were gradually released. British territories overseas also interned foreign nationals during World War II.

INTERNATIONAL COMMITTEE OF THE RED CROSS

Few records about internees are held in TNA, as the British government passed information to the International Committee of the Red Cross in Geneva. This organization has compiled records of prisoners of war and internees from all nations during both World Wars. Researchers cannot consult these, but the Red Cross will supply information in response to written requests and the payment of a fee. At TNA there is also a list of internees' names and an index to World War II internees.

FURTHER HELP

Commonwealth War Graves
  Commission, 2 Marlow Road,
  Maidenhead, Berkshire SL6 7DX.
The Debt of Honour Register, listing
  those killed and where they are
  buried (if known) during the two
  World Wars, is available on
  CD-ROM and on the website
  www.cwgc.org
TNA Factsheets:
  *Armed Forces records held in
    the UK*
  *British Army nurses' service records
    1914–18*
  *British Prisoners of the Second World
    War and Korean War*

British Prisoners of War c.1790–1919
Board of Ordnance
Civilian gallantry medals
Conscientious Objectors
Intelligence and Security Services
Internees
Military nursing
*Prisoners of war interview reports
  1914–1918*
Prisoners of war in British Hands
Victoria Cross registers 1856–1944
Ingham, Mary *Tracing Your Service
  Women Ancestors* (Pen & Sword)
Tomaselli, Phil *Tracing Your Secret
  Service Ancestors* (Pen & Sword)

Army records

Before 1660, there was no standing army: soldiers were recruited as the need arose. Each regiment was generally known by the name of the colonel who commanded it, until the early 18th century, when they acquired more permanent names. Since then, the Army has been reorganized several times, and regiments have been renamed and amalgamated. There are histories of the Army and individual regiments that will help researchers.

FOREIGN SOLDIERS
Men from many different nationalities joined the Army, but, in addition, there were regiments composed of foreign soldiers commanded by white British officers. The most famous is the brigade of Gurkhas, originally formed in 1815, which comprises soldiers recruited from Nepal in North

ABOVE Cavalry troops took part in battles until World War I.

BELOW Armies depend on men willing to die for their country's cause.

> **The structure of the Army**
>
> Brigade
> Battalion/regiment
> Company
> Platoon/troop
>
> Cavalry are mounted troops
> Infantry are foot soldiers

India. Others were the West Africa Regiments, raised from 1800, and the West Indian Regiments, from 1795. The latter had their origins in the Carolina Black Corps established in America during the War of Independence. On the independence of their various countries, the West African and West Indian regiments ceased to be part of the British Army.

ABOVE Women and children were among the "camp followers" who went on military campaigns with the army.

WOMEN IN THE ARMY

Women didn't officially join the Army until 1949, when the Women's Royal Army Corps (WRAC) was formed, although there had been a few women's units in World War I. As long as there were soldiers, however, there were women, including wives, accompanying them. They were called camp followers, and they did the laundry, nursed casualties and provided other services. This was semi-acknowledged: the Army kept records of births of children to serving soldiers whose wives were attached to the regiment while on a campaign. Surviving registers from 1761 are in TNA and have been indexed.

RECRUITMENT AND TRAINING

Until 1871, commissioned officers were almost exclusively drawn from the upper classes or wealthy families, because they had to pay for their appointments and promotion. Non-commissioned officers came up through the ranks. Conscription was introduced only in World War I. Before that, recruiting officers toured the country to encourage young men to join the Army. Criminals might also be offered the option of joining up, especially in wartime.

Until the establishment of the various Army colleges, beginning in 1802 with officer training, any instruction needed was given by the unit to which a soldier was posted. As equipment became more specialized, especially in the 20th century, apprenticeships were offered to those wishing to acquire a particular skill.

LOCATING ARMY RECORDS

Finding and putting together records relating to Army ancestors is not easy: this is a highly specialized area of research. Although there are many records (mainly pre-20th century) in TNA, individual regiments may have their own archives and many also have museums where papers may be lodged. There is also the National Army Museum in London. Many records relating to soldiers in the World Wars

Army ranks

Commissioned officers
Field Marshal
General
Lieutenant General
Major General
Brigadier
Colonel
Lieutenant Colonel
Major
Captain
Lieutenant
Second Lieutenant
Non-commissioned officers and other ranks
Warrant Officer 1st class
(Regimental Sergeant Major)
Warrant Officer 2nd class
(Company Sergeant Major)
Sergeant Major
Staff Sergeant
Sergeant
Corporal
Lance Corporal
Private (also called a Gunner in the Artillery, a Sapper in the Engineers and a Trooper in the Cavalry)

Significant dates in the history of the Army

Note that the establishment and name changes of all the different regiments, as well as many support departments, have been omitted.

1660/1 Standing army established.
1716 First separate artillery regiment created.
1717 Corps of Engineers formed.
1741 Royal Military Academy created at Woolwich, East London, initially to train artillery officers and later engineers and signals personnel.
1796 Chaplains' Department formed.

1802 Royal Military College created at Great Marlow and later moved to Sandhurst, Berkshire, to train officers of the cavalry and infantry divisions.
1857 Military Music School (currently Royal Military School of Music) created at Kneller Hall, Middlesex.
1858 Staff College created at Camberley, Surrey.
1858 Veterinary Medical Department (currently the Royal Army Veterinary Corps) formed.
1877 Military police introduced.
1897 Army Nursing Service (currently Queen Alexandra's Royal Army Nursing Corps) formed.
1916 Tanks introduced into warfare.
1920 Separate Corps of Signals created.
1939 Conscription introduced.
1940 First Parachute Corps formed.
1947 National Service introduced (abolished in 1961).
1947 Royal Military Academy amalgamated with the Royal Military College at Sandhurst.
1949 Women's Royal Army Corps (WRACS) formed.
1952 Special Air Service Regiment formed.

ABOVE Flags, furled while marching, provide a rallying point for soldiers who have become lost or cut off from their comrades on the battlefield. The crests on the flags originated in the days when most people could not read.

were destroyed by bombing. The majority of recent records are still with the Ministry of Defence; they are not on open access, and a fee is charged for research. The family historian researching a soldier ancestor must therefore find out where he served and, for both World Wars, his service number, if possible.

ABOVE A studio photograph like this was often taken before a soldier went abroad.

FURTHER HELP

The website of the Army Museums Ogilby Trust has links to British Army museums in the UK www.armymuseums.org.uk

The histories of individual regiments can be found on the British Army's website: www.army.mod.uk/infantry/regiments

TNA has factsheets on:
Army regiments
British Army Officers after 1913
British Army Soldiers after 1913
British Army Operations up to 1913
British Army Operations in the First World War
British Army Operations in the Second World War
British Army operations after 1945
British military campaign and service medals
British military gallantry records
British Prisoners of War c. 1790-1919
Courts martial and desertion in the British army 17th-20th centuries

Disability and dependents' pensions in the First World War
Women in the British Army
Women's Army Auxiliary Corps service records 1917-1929

Duckers, Peter, *British Campaign Medals* (Shire Books)

Fowler, Simon *Tracing Your First World War Ancestors* (Countryside Books)

Fowler, Simon *Tracing Your Second World War Ancestors* (Countryside Books)

Spencer, William *Army Records: a guide for family historians* (TNA)

Spencer, William *Medals; the researcher's guide* (TNA)

Watts, Michael & Watts, Christopher *My Ancestor was in the Army* (SoG)

The Naval & Military Press specialises in books about the armed forces www.naval-military-press.com

Royal Air Force records

The Royal Air Force (RAF) was created comparatively recently, and so researching family members who served in it can be simpler than working on other branches of the armed forces. By the beginning of the 20th century, bureaucrats were better at record-keeping, and there are fewer records to search.

THE BEGINNING OF AERIAL WARFARE

As early as 1804, experiments using balloons were being conducted at the Royal Military Academy in Woolwich, London, and they were used in wars in Africa and China at the end of the 19th century. There was even a School of Ballooning at Aldershot, Hampshire. These balloons came under the responsibility of the Royal Engineers, which were part of the British Army, so any records relating to ancestors who worked with them will be in Army records.

It was not long after the first flight in a heavier-than-air machine in 1903 that the potential for aeroplanes and,

ABOVE Royal Airforce pilots in an overseas airfield in 1964. A photograph such as this in a family member's archives might be where your research in military records begins.

later, airships in warfare was recognized. On 1 April 1918, the Royal Air Force was formed by the amalgamation of the Royal Flying Corps and the Royal Naval Air Service.

The RAF is divided into commands – different sections responsible for particular types of activity. There are currently only two (Strike Command, and Personnel and Training Command),

but in the past there were more, such as Bomber Command, Fighter Command, Training Command, etc. Each of these Commands contained a number of groups, divided into squadrons. A squadron consisted of a number of airplanes, the crews (pilots, navigators, gunners and signallers) who flew in them and the ground crew who maintained and repaired them. The airfields

RAF ranks

Commissioned officers
Marshal of the Royal Air Force
Air Chief Marshal
Air Marshal
Air Vice-Marshal
Air Commodore
Group Captain
Wing Commander
Squadron Leader
Flight Lieutenant
Flying Officer, Pilot Officer

Non-commissioned officers and other ranks
Warrant Officer/Master Aircrew
Flight Sergeant
Sergeant
Corporal
Senior Aircraftman/woman
Leading Aircraftman/woman
Senior Technician
Junior Technician

ABOVE The shark's mouth was a motif used by 211 squadron in World War II.

Significant dates in the history of the RAF

1912 Royal Naval Air Service (RNAS) and Royal Flying Corps (RFC) established.
1918 RNAS and RFC merged to form Royal Air Force (RAF).
1918 RAF Nursing Service created, becoming Princess Mary's RAF Nursing Service in 1923.
1918 Women's Royal Air Force (WRAF) created (abolished in 1920).
1920 RAF College opened at Cranwell.
1939 Women's Auxiliary Air Force (WAAF) created.
1994 WAAF integrated into the RAF.

from which they flew also needed medical and administrative staff, stores, transport – all the usual back-up involved in any large organization.

WRAF AND WAAF

The Women's Royal Air Force (WRAF) was formed at the same time as the Royal Air Force in 1918. It was disbanded in 1920, but re-established as the Women's Auxiliary Air Force (WAAF) in 1939. In World War I, the role of women was confined to administration, but in World War II they did work in some technical and mechanical grades as well. They were not allowed to join operational aircrews, although there were women pilots in Ferry Command and the Air Transport Auxiliary (ATA), which flew aircraft from one place to another.

Very few records relating to women officers from World War I have survived, although ordinary airwomen's records are in TNA, where there is an index to all Air Force personnel, which includes women, and gives service numbers.

RESEARCH AND DEVELOPMENT

The government played a great part in the research, development and manufacture of aircraft, airships and radar systems. Many of the records are in TNA, and the RAF Museum also has a substantial collection, as well as many old aircraft.

NURSING SERVICES

At the outbreak of World War I, advertisements were placed in nursing journals to recruit personnel for the Royal Air Force Nursing Service (RAFNS). At first this service was intended to last only as long as the hostilities, but after the war the government decided to make it a permanent part of the RAF. In 1923, it became Princess Mary's Royal Air Force Nursing Service.

If your ancestors were among the very first volunteers, information about them might be in TNA, which mainly holds documents relating to the establishment of the RAFNS and the decision to continue it. Otherwise their records will be with the RAF.

ABOVE Nursing staff on an exercise to learn to help air crash victims.

LOCATING RAF RECORDS

Records relating to servicemen whose service number was between 1 and 329000 (largely those who served in the RAF during World War I) are mainly in TNA, where there is an index of service numbers. The records of anyone who was still serving in the RAF at the outbreak of World War II, however, will still be with RAF's records.

The RAF Museum at Hendon, North London, holds many records, including log books and officers' diaries, as well as a card index of every aircraft belonging to the RAF.

FURTHER HELP

TNA Factsheets are available on:
RAF, RFC and RNAS personnel after 1913
Royal Air Force combat reports 1939-1945
Royal Air Force nurses
Royal Air Force officers' service records 1918-1919
Royal Air Force operations
Royal Air Force operations record books 1939-1945
Royal Air Force squadrons
Research and development in the

Royal Air Force
Women's Royal Air Force personnel
Women's Royal Air Force service records 1918-1920
Spencer William *Air Force Records for Family Historians* (TNA)
Tomaselli, Phil *Tracing Your Air Force Ancestors* (Pen & Sword)
The Royal Air Force Museums has reprints of some early training manuals www.rafmuseum.org.uk
RAF website has a history of the service with videos, www.raf.mod.uk

Royal Navy records

Known as the Senior Service, the Navy is the longest-established branch of the armed services, having its roots in the 9th century. There are some medieval and Tudor records relating to it, but most date from the post-Commonwealth period. Samuel Pepys, the famous diarist, was from 1660 a civil servant who rose to the top of the Navy Board. He reformed many aspects of naval practice and introduced many of the systems that survive today. He also laid down methods of record keeping for which the genealogist should be grateful.

ABOVE The *Henry Addington*, festooned with flags of many nations, fires her guns on a ceremonial occasion in 1802 at West India Docks, London.

SECTIONS OF THE ROYAL NAVY

The Royal Navy (RN) is divided into four sections: Ships, Royal Marines, Fleet Air Arm and Submarines. In addition, there is the Women's Royal Naval Service, which has formed a permanent part of the Royal Navy since 1939.

Ships

The history of the vessels themselves is largely one of developments in technology, as ships changed from being made of wood to metal. They were first powered by sails, then steam, then diesel, and, in the case of submarines, nuclear power. With the changes in technology came the need for more specialized and trained personnel, which led to a variety of job titles.

Royal Marines

The Marines were originally soldiers who served at sea. They were founded in 1664 as the Admiral's Regiment. In 1755 they came under the control of the Admiralty and were, like sailors, entitled to enter the Greenwich Hospital after discharge.

The Marines, first formed in 1755, had four divisions, depending on where they were based, and they usually remained with the same division throughout their career. The first three bases were Chatham, Portsmouth and Plymouth, and during 1805–69 the fourth was at Woolwich. Records for 1793–1925 are in TNA, but those relating to officers after 1925 are held at the Royal Marines' Historical Office. There are also some 20th-century records in the Fleet Air Arm Museum. The Royal Marines

---

Navy ranks

There are a bewildering number of titles and ranks in the Royal Navy, which have changed over the years. The following is an abbreviated list.

Commissioned officers
Admiral
Commodore
Captain
Commander
Lieutenant
Mate/Sub-lieutenant
Master (after 1808)
Midshipman

Other ranks
Warrant Officer
Boatswain/Bosun
Gunner
Carpenter
Chaplain
Purser
Schoolmaster (18th century)/
Naval instructor
Cook
Rating (the ordinary seaman)

Museum at Southsea also has many documents, diaries and other records relating to individuals' experiences.

Fleet Air Arm

This section of the Navy is responsible for aircraft of all kinds launched from on board ship. In World War I, it also operated armoured cars transported by ship to the battlefields.

Submarines

The first British submarine was launched in 1901, and by the outbreak of World War II there were 74 submarines in service.

Women in the Royal Navy

From early times, women were frequently, but unofficially, found on board ship. Between the mid-17th century and the mid-19th century, warrant officers were allowed to take their wives to sea, but they rarely appear in the muster books. During battles, women carried ammunition and tended to the wounded. Petitions requesting financial help if their husbands were killed in action and as recompense for their own work as nurses may be found at TNA.

Reports of women disguising themselves as men to serve on board ship are occasionally found. They were immediately discharged when their gender was discovered. It was not until World War I that the Women's Royal Naval Service (WRNS – pronounced "Wrens") was formed. It lasted only a year (1918–19) but was reformed in 1939 for World War II.

MUSTER BOOKS

Ships' muster books, to be found in TNA, list all members of a crew on a particular ship when it began a new voyage, and this is the main way of tracing a rating's career. Ships had to take their support services with them, and so, in addition to the officers and sailors, crews would include surgeons, chaplains, cooks and carpenters, who might all be found in muster books.

Until 1853, commissioned officers and sailors were paid off at the end of each voyage, although warrant officers were generally regarded as belonging to a particular ship. Officers were put on half-pay until they received a new commission, but the ratings had to fend for themselves. Many ratings would try to remain in the service of a particular captain because they had become accustomed and loyal to him.

APPRENTICESHIPS

Before 1794, naval officers could begin an apprenticeship when they were only 7 years old. They were generally known as midshipmen, and after a period of on-the-job training and study in navigational skills, they passed an examination to qualify as a lieutenant. Ships usually had someone on board to educate children and

---

Significant dates in the history of the Navy

As an island, England has always needed ships for defence, so the Navy's origins pre-date the Norman Conquest.
1642 Permanent Navy structure established.
1652 Creation of the post of "able" seaman, senior to and more experienced than the "ordinary" kind.
1660 Samuel Pepys became Clerk of the Acts at the Navy Board. Between this date and his resignation in 1689, by which time he had been promoted to Secretary of the Admiralty, he created an administrative system that lasted into the 19th century.
1694 Foundation of Greenwich Hospital.

1733 Royal Naval Academy founded (became Royal Naval College in 1806).
1755 Royal Marines transfer from Army to Navy control.
1795 Issue of lemon juice to prevent scurvy introduced.
1820 RN began surveying and mapping the seas.
1824 First attempts to standardize uniforms.
1825 Rum ration halved.
1831 Beer ration abolished.
1830 Gunnery School created.
1835 Register of Seamen introduced.
1840s Steam-powered ships introduced, requiring stokers to feed coal into the engines.
1859 Royal Naval Reserve established.

1871 Flogging in peacetime suspended (1879 suspended totally, but not actually abolished).
1873 Royal Naval College transferred to Greenwich.
1880 Royal Naval Engineering College opened.
1901 Submarines introduced.
1903 Osborne section of the Royal Naval College opened on the Isle of Wight.
1918 Women's Royal Navy Service (WRNS) created.
1937 Fleet Air Arm transferred from RAF to RN control.
1963 First nuclear-powered submarine introduced.
1994 WRNS integrated into the RN.

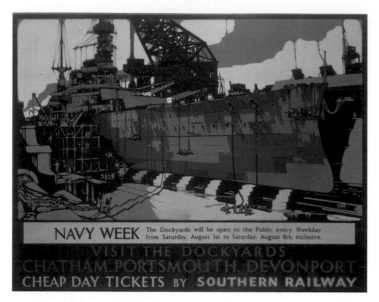

NAVY WEEK The Dockyards will be open to the Public every Weekday from Saturday, August 1st to Saturday, August 8th, inclusive.

VISIT THE DOCKYARDS
CHATHAM, PORTSMOUTH, DEVONPORT
CHEAP DAY TICKETS BY SOUTHERN RAILWAY

ABOVE Devoting a whole week to celebrating the Navy shows how important it was in the nation's consciousness in the 1930s.

young sailors. From the early 19th century, some chaplains were also acting as schoolmasters. Warrant officers could also become lieutenants. Promotion thereafter was largely through ability, though the patronage of senior officers was also essential. Midshipmen received certificates, called Passing Certificates, on becoming qualified, and these are held at TNA.

ROYAL NAVAL COLLEGE

A training school for young naval officers was founded at Dartmouth in 1863. It was initially based in two hulks moored on the River Dart, but in 1905 a college was built. The junior section of the Royal Naval College was set up at Osborne on the Isle of Wight to educate boys who would progress to the College at Dartmouth.

As well as attracting the sons of the middle and upper classes, who were sent there to learn to be officers, the Navy provided a convenient way of providing for orphans, and various organizations and charities sent boys into the service.

PRESS GANGS AND THE ROYAL NAVAL RESERVE

Although attracting naval officers was relatively easy, it was not quite as simple to get ordinary sailors, or ratings, to serve. In times of war, young men condemned to death for a crime might be offered the alternative of enrolling in the Navy, and men might be legally pressed into service, which was effectively kidnapping.

Not all men were in danger of this, however, because the last thing the Navy needed was those who were unaccustomed to the sea and who might imperil their fellow sailors or the ship through seasickness or ignorance. Press-ganged landlubbers were therefore usually released if taken on board, while the press gangs went in search of merchant seamen and fishermen. If an

ancestor working in a marine occupation suddenly disappears, this may be because his ship sank, but it might also be because he was press-ganged into the Navy, so it is worth checking out both possibilities.

Local papers in maritime areas might report riots or fights caused by people trying to prevent their menfolk being taken. This might also have led to criminal proceedings.

After 1859, this unusual recruiting practice was regularized through the formation of the Royal Naval Reserve, whereby merchant seamen could be called up into the Royal Navy as the need arose.

NAVAL DOCKYARDS

Naval dockyards, where ships were built and equipped, employed a range of skilled workmen: shipwrights, ropemakers, carpenters, and so forth, as well as general labourers. The ships also had to take their food with them. Both sections came under the ultimate authority of the Admiralty. Supplying guns, however, came under the Board of Ordnance. Surviving records for Britain date from the late 18th century. In addition to establishments in Britain, the Navy maintained dockyards all over the world, and some of these records go back to the beginning of the 18th century.

RESEARCH AND DEVELOPMENT

Most naval R&D was carried out by private firms under the patronage of the Admiralty. It is possible that some information may exist in company archives, but, since the development of ships and weapons would have been confidential, most records will be in TNA. Patents on inventions before 1853 are also held in TNA. After that they are with the Patent Office.

GREENWICH HOSPITAL

The Greenwich Hospital was opened in 1694 and closed in 1869. Until then, seamen who had served in the Royal Navy (but not the Merchant Navy) were entitled to live there. The rules were stringent – basically no wine, women or song – so many sailors who had reached retirement age or had been invalided out of the Navy chose to live outside but still collect their naval pensions. The records are in TNA.

LOCATING RECORDS OF THE ROYAL NAVY

Printed lists of officers were published as the Navy List during 1782–1914. Records relating to officers entering the service after 1890 and ratings after 1892 remain with the Ministry of Defence Royal Navy records. Before that date, most are in TNA. The National Maritime Museum holds a

large collection of naval portraits and photographs of ships and sailors. The Royal Naval Museum holds many private documents, pictures and photographs, donated by former and serving men and their families, which date back to the late 18th century. These show what life at sea was like over the years.

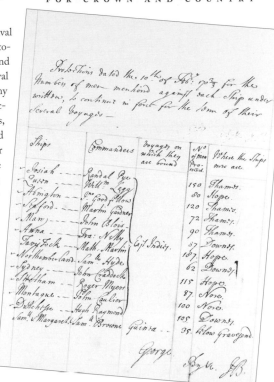

RIGHT Lists were kept of those protected from being press-ganged.

FURTHER HELP

TNA has fact sheets on personnel in both the Royal Navy and the Merchant Navy. They include:
Fleet Air Arm personnel
How to find Royal Navy ships' voyages in log books
Royal Marines officers
Royal Marines other ranks
Royal Marines service records 1842–1925
Royal Naval Air Service officers
Royal Naval Air Service ratings
Royal Naval Division personnel
Royal Naval Division service records 1914–1919
Royal Naval dockyard staff
Royal Naval Reserve personnel
Royal Naval Reserve service records 1860–1955
Royal Naval Volunteer Reserve personnel
Royal Naval Volunteer Reserve personnel 1903–1922
Royal Naval Volunteer Reserve service records 1903–1922

Royal Navy commissioned and warrant officers
Royal Navy commissioned and warrant officers: further research
Royal Navy nurses
Royal Navy officers' service record cards and files c. 1840–c.1920
Royal Navy officers' service records 1756–1931
Royal Navy officers pensions
Royal Navy ratings 1853–1923
Royal Navy ratings after1923
Royal Navy ratings before 1853
Royal Navy ratings: further research
Royal Navy ratings' pensions
Royal Navy ratings' service records 1853–1923
Royal Navy warrant officers
Wills of Royal Navy warrant officers and ratings 1786–1882
Women's Royal Naval Service personnel
Women's Royal Naval Service records 1917–1919
And many more......

Merchant Navy
Crew lists, agreements and log books of merchant ships 1747–1860
Crew lists, agreements and log books of merchant ships after 1861
Merchant seamen serving after 1917
Merchant seamen serving 1858–1917
Merchant seamen serving up to 1857
Merchant seamen's campaign medal records 1914–1918
Merchant seamen's medals and honours
Officers in the Merchant Navy

Cock, Randolph & Rodger, N.A.M. A *Guide to the Naval Records in the National Archives of the UK* (Institute of Historical Research/National Archives of the UK)
Watts, Michael & Watts, Christopher *My Ancestor was a Merchant Seaman* (SoG)
Divall, Ken *My Ancestor was a Royal Marine* (SoG)

Lifecycle checklist

On the opposite page is a list of the events that occur in most people's lives. It is included as a reminder of the kinds of records the family historian needs to look for, with an indication of where they are most likely to be found. Of course there is no such thing as an "average" life – everyone's is different in some way from the norm – but the following points may help in your research.

ADOLESCENCE

Men were at their most mobile between the ages of 15 and 21, at the time of taking up apprenticeships or beginning work. They also moved the greatest distance during this period in their lives. In Victorian times, servants aged 12–15 were the most mobile of all male workers.

MARRIAGE

Contrary to popular belief, our ancestors rarely married before the age of 20. There were child marriages (or, more precisely, betrothals), but these were arranged between landowners for financial and dynastic purposes, and the couples concerned rarely lived together until they were in their mid- to late teens.

In the early 17th century, the average age at first marriage was 28 for men and 25 for women. These figures dropped over the 18th century, and by the beginning of the 19th century they were 26 and 24 respectively. By the early 20th century they had fallen again, but since the last quarter of the 20th century they have been rising again. These figures seem to have been linked to economic factors, such as

industrialization, which meant that young people could earn a comparatively good wage at a younger age. Couples waited until they had accumulated enough money to set up a separate home – multi-generational households, or those consisting of extended families, were rare. A widowed parent might live with a child and in-law, especially in industrial areas where women needed to work, and would provide childcare.

Marriage was the time at which women were at their most mobile. Although they tended to marry in their home parish, they usually went to live in their husband's place of residence. Most couples lived within 32km (20 miles) of each other, presumably because they met at fairs and markets, and 16km (10 miles) was about the limit of how far people were prepared to walk.

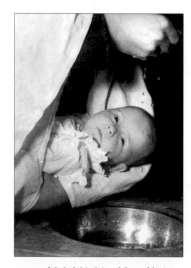

ABOVE A baby's birth is celebrated by its family, and recorded by the state.

FAMILY SIZE

The high death rate among babies and young children in the late 18th century meant that the average number of children a couple could expect to survive was six. This number had dropped to five in the mid-19th century. By the 1920s the average number of children in a family was just two, but this figure represents a deliberate decision to limit family size rather than a massive growth in child mortality.

LIFE EXPECTANCY

Until the 20th century, the average life expectancy at birth was roughly 30–40 years at different times during the preceding centuries. This apparently low figure is because so many babies died in the first two years of life. A person who survived to the age of 20 could, however, expect to live to 50; at 30, people could expect to reach 60; and those who survived to 60 had a good chance of reaching 70 or even 80. A few then achieved 90 or even 100. These figures were for the country as a whole, disguising the difference between a relatively wholesome life in the country and life in cities, which, until the Victorian era brought improved sanitation, was dangerous.

Clean water, efficient sewage disposal systems and better personal hygiene had a greater effect on increasing life expectancy than advances in medical treatment until the last half of the 20th century. The introduction of antibiotics after World War II brought the next leap in public health improvement. Further advances mean that today more and more people live to 100 years and beyond.

From the cradle to the grave

AGE	EVENT	RECORDS	LOCATION OF RECORDS
0	BIRTH	After 1837 – birth certificate	TNA
		Before 1837 – parish registers	CRO
0+	BAPTISM	Church of England parish registers	CRO
		Nonconformist churches	TNA or CRO
		Roman Catholic churches	Church or DRO
4-18	SCHOOL	Public schools	Published or with school
		Church schools	CRO/denominational archives
		Local Education Authority	CRO
14+	UNIVERSITY	Alumni lists	Published
14-21	APPRENTICESHIP	Indentures	Private papers
		1710–1811 Apprenticeship tax records	TNA
		Poor Law records (for parish apprentices)	CRO
7+	WORK	Directories	Published
		Censuses	TNA
	PROFESSIONS	Published lists/membership of professional bodies	Libraries
	BUSINESS	Company archives	Libraries/CRO
	ARTISANS	Guild membership	CRO
7+	MILITARY SERVICE	Service records	TNA/museums
15+	MILITIA SERVICE	Militia ballot	CRO
		Pay and musters	TNA
	VOLUNTEERS	Pay and musters	TNA/CRO
21+	PROPERTY	Deeds	TNA/CRO
	ACQUISITION	Ratebooks	CRO
		Directories	Published
	FRANCHISE	Poll books	Published
		Electoral registers	CRO/British Library
12/14+	MARRIAGE	After 1837 – marriage certificate	TNA
		1753–1837 – Anglican parish church	CRO
		Before 1753 – denominational church	CRO/TNA
		Marriage licence	CRO/DRO
	CHILDREN	After 1837 – birth certificate	TNA
		Before 1837 – church records	CRO
		Illegitimate children – bastardy examinations	CRO
	LEGAL	Crime	CRO/TNA
	PROCEEDINGS	Property disputes	TNA
	INTERNAL	Settlement certificates/examinations	CRO
	MIGRATION	Removal orders	CRO
	EMIGRATION		
	Voluntary	Government schemes	TNA
	Transportation	Crime and prison records	TNA/CRO
	ILLNESS	Hospital records	CRO/other repositories
		Workhouse records	CRO
	DEATH	After 1837 – death certificate	TNA
		Before 1837 – burial registers	CRO/TNA
		Obituaries in newspapers/periodicals	CRO/British Library
	INQUEST	Coroners' records	CRO/TNA
		Newspaper reports	CRO/British Library
	WILL	After 1858	Probate Registry
		Before 1858	CRO/DRO/TNA

Effective research on the internet

The explosion of information on the internet means that there are an infinite number of books and websites available. The following selection of websites are a useful starting point.

General Sources
Genfair, at www.genfair.co.uk, and S&N Genealogy, at www.genealogsupplies.com, specialise in family and local history material.

Ancestry, at www.ancestry.co.uk, is a commerical website that offers an online service to help you draw up a family tree. Electoral registers, parish records as far back as 1538, census, and BMD certificates are indexed there.

On the Electoral Registers website, www.electoralregisters.org.uk, there is information about elections, links to free online sources, and a list of Poll Books from 1700–1872.

The BBC's family history website has useful links for the beginner at www.bbc.co.uk/history/familyhistory.

The Federation of Family History Societies website has pay-per-view parish registers, memorial inscriptions, census transcriptions and more, at www.familyhistoryonline.net.

Military and apprentice records, wills, parish records and much more for the UK can be found on the Origins site, www.originsnetwork.com.

Genes Reunited, www.genesreunited.co.uk, is a commercial site with some census and other records online. It also has noticeboards for those looking for family members .

Family Relatives, www.familyrelatives.com, is a commercial site, which is strong on sources relating to Australia and New Zealand.

Access to Archives (A2A) contains the catalogues of record offices in England and Wales www.nationalarchives.gov.uk/a2a

Author, Peter Christian, has put his *Web Publishing for Genealogy* online, at www.spub.co.uk.

A free Open University course on Victorian photography called Picturing the Family can be found on www.open.ac.uk.

Jayne Shrimpton runs a service to help date photographs on www.jayneshrimpton.co.uk.

Pharos Teaching & Tutoring Ltd, www.pharostutors.com, runs online courses for genealogists.

BMD Certificates
For GRO BMD indexes, go to: www.bmdindex.co.uk.

For records of birth, baptism, marriage, death and burial taken from non-parochial sources, mainly nonconformist churches, but also the registry of shipping and seamen 1854-1908, go to www.bmdregisters.co.uk.

The National Burial Index, a volunteer project by the FFHS, is a database of entries recorded in English and Welsh burials registers – parish, nonconformist, Roman Catholic, Quaker and cemetery – mainly after 1815. Coverage is not yet complete. Available on Findmypast and on CD-Rom in many libraries and record offices.

Deceased Online is a database, in progress, of burial and cemetery records in the UK and Republic of Ireland: go to www.deceasedonline.com.

For BMD of shipping and seamen 1854–1908, and other overseas events go to www.bmdregisters.co.uk.

For adopted relatives' BMD, go to the Adoption Section, Room C202, General Register Office, Trafalgar Road, Southport PR8 2HH; www.gov.uk/adoption-records

Censuses
Go to www.freecen.org.uk, a voluntary input site for census returns.

Inquests
For coroners' records 1690–1800, go to London Lives, useful for everyone, not just London ancestors: www.londonlives.org/static/IC.jsp.

Published material
Old books that are now out of print and without copyright restriction can be found online from several websites. The major ones are Project Gutenberg at www.gutenberg.org and Google Books at www.books.google.co.uk.

Academic libraries, especially in America, also have digitized copies of old books online.

WorldCat, at www.worldcat.org, is a database with the holdings of thousands of libraries, so you can see if what you want is on line or if libraries near you own the book.

Shire Books publishes booklets detailing the history of various industries. They also have general histories of institutions, like hospitals or almshouses where an ancestor might have worked at www.shirebooks.co.uk.

Industrial museums or historical re-enactments are helpful if you want some background into how a trade or skill was carried out. The National Association of Re-enactment Societies website is www.nares.org.uk

Wills

For information about obtaining wills after 1858, go to: www.justice.gov.uk/about/hmcts.

Scottish Records

The National Records of Scotland, www.nrscotland.gov.uk, holds BMD records, tax rolls, census and wills.

Welsh Records

Start with the Association of Family History Societies of Wales at: www.fhswales.org.uk. There is an online index of mariners and engineers from 1800 to 1945 at www.welsh-mariners.org.uk.

Irish Records

Try the Representative Church Body at www.ireland.anglican.org. There is also a searchable database of Irish (and Canadian) merchant seamen 1918–1921 on www.irishmariners.ie.

Isle of Man Records

Genealogy Pages Isle of Man has information about different sources and some transcribed records, e.g. a list of householders in Douglas in 1730, www.isle-of-man.com/manxnote-book/famhist/genealgy [sic].

Educational Institutions

For schools run by religious denominations go to The Baptist Research Library, www.rpc.ox.ac.uk for a list of what they have archived, or the British & Foreign School Society Archives, www.bfss.org.uk/archive.

For Dr Williams's Library, the most important research library for English Protestant nonconformity, (Congregationalists, English Presbyterians and Unitarians), go to www.dwlib.co.uk.

Sources related to Methodist history are among the special collections in the John Rylands University, Library of Manchester, at www.library.manchester.ac.uk/rylands.

For United Reformed Church records (and the Presbyterian Church of England), go to www.westminster.cam.ac.uk.

Archives of Catholic schools are usually held with the local diocesan records, or with the schools. For a list of dioceses, go to www.r-c.org.uk.

Included in the miscellaneous information on Mary Wall's Missing Ancestors website, www.missing-ancestors.com, is a database of pupils at industrial and reform schools.

The Children's Society's Hidden Lives Revealed website, www.hidden-lives.org.uk, relates to children in care from 1881-1981, has useful background information and some records from its early archives.

Professional Records

For medical staff go to the Hospital Records Database of the NA, www.nationalarchives.gov.uk/hospital records, which lists the location and contents of records relating to hospitals in the UK (usually closed for 100 years). Or The Royal College of Nursing archives at www.rcn.org.uk/development/rcn_archives.

The Wellcome Institute for the History of Medicine has an outstanding collection of books and records, including papers from doctors and hospitals at www.wellcome.ac.uk.

The Clergy of the Church of England Database 1540–1835, www.theclergydatabase.org.uk, makes available the principal records of ecclesiastical careers from over 50 archives in England and Wales. If your ordained ancestor spent time overseas, try the Mundus Gateway, a web-based guide to over 400 overseas missionary materials, www.mundus.ac.uk. The Surman index to Congregationalist and other ministers 1600–1972 in Dr Williams' Library is on www.dwlib.co.uk.

Transcripts of trials at the Old Bailey (1674–1913) at www.oldbaileyonline.org.uk may include a police ancestor who gave evidence. The Police History Society website, www.policehistorysociety.co.uk, has links to individual forces' websites, which may include the locality of their archives.

The Royal Human Society's website, www.royalhumanesociety.org.uk, has a database of medals awarded by the Society.

For post office employees go to The British Postal Museum and Archive, www.postalheritage.org.uk.

For railway workers go to the National Railway Museum, Library Archive in York on www.nrm.org.uk.

Military Personnel

Forces War Records, www.forces-war-records.co.uk, a commercial site, holds over 4 million military records going back to before 1630. The National Army Museum, www.nam.ac.uk, has the Templer Study Centre for the history of the British Army. It does not contain soldiers' records, but there is a family history page with useful links.

For The Royal Air Force Museum, go to www.rafmuseum.org.uk, The Fleet Air Arm Archive 1939–45 www.fleetairarmarchive.net, or The Fleet Air Arm Museum, at www.fleetairarm.com.

For The Royal Marines Museum, go towww.royalmarinesmuseum.co.uk.

For the Royal Naval Museum, go to www.royalnavalmuseum.org, or The Royal Navy Submarine Museum, at www.submarine-museum.co.uk. The National Maritime Museum, Greenwich, London, www.nmm.ac.uk, contains the Caird Library for the history of the Royal Navy but it does not have individual sailors' records.

Index